"I have known Dr. Woodworth for a long time. He is a very thoughtful, talented human being. His book *Kisses from Heaven* is exactly that: It's all about what we can learn from the Good Lord and apply to our lives. A wonderful spiritual read!"

—**Ken Blanchard**, Coauthor,
The New One-Minute Manager
and *Lead Like Jesus Revisited*

"Dr. Woodworth is one of my heroes. He heard the Lord and helped save my wife's life when she was diagnosed with cerebral malaria after a trip to Uganda. It's hard to imagine what would have happened if he wasn't in tune with the Holy Spirit. This book will build your faith in Jesus, encourage believers, bring prodigals home, save the lost, and give glory to our Father. We all can hear His voice; this book will encourage you to believe it is true in your own life."

—**Mike Salley**, Founder/Executive Director,
Show Mercy International

"Great read! Highly recommended—I couldn't put this one down! Great mix of aeronautical moments, medical emergency challenges, and missionary miracles. A delightful true-life commentary on Romans 8:14, 'being led by the Spirit.' God's amazing love carries the book from beginning to end."

—**Pastor Phil Freeman**, Author,
Miracle Moments: Holy Spirit Action in Our Day

"I have known C.B. Caleb Woodworth for ten years, and he and his wife have become very close friends. They walk their talk and are true examples of how Christians should live. In Matthew 3:11, John the Baptist says, 'I indeed baptize you with water unto repentance. But he that cometh after me is mightier than I, whose shoes I am not worthy to bear: he shall baptize you with the Holy Ghost, and with fire.' My friends live this scripture. They are born-again Chrisitans, baptized in the Holy Ghost and with fire, and you will find this statement to be true as you read their book *Kisses from Heaven*."

—**Reverend Bob Rice, D.D.**, Church Planter, Evangelist

"*Kisses from Heaven* is a book that shows you not to fear God's leading. The author lets you into his life, his never-ending service to the Lord, his willingness to go anywhere God leads him, and his devotion to let God send him three feet from hell if he could share the gospel and rescue one person from the devil's pit. You cannot get far into this book without saying, 'Here I am Lord, send me.'"

—**Jeanie Selby**, Author, *And I Will Declare His Greatness*

A TRILOGY OF
GOD'S STORIES

Kisses
from
Heaven

BOOK ONE

*Unique, Inexplicable, Extraordinary,
and Supernatural Tales from the
Heart of a Miraculous God*

"Publish His glorious deeds among the nations. Tell
everyone about the amazing things He does."
—Psalm 96:3, NLT

C. B. Caleb Woodworth, MD
with *My Dear Wife and Co-author, Emily Woodworth*

Kisses from Heaven: Unique, Inexplicable, Extraordinary, and Supernatural Tales from the Heart of a Miraculous God
A Trilogy of God's Stories, Book One

The cover was designed using assets by studio4rt from Freepik.com.
Book design by Inspire Books

Scripture quotations taken from the (NASB®) New American Standard Bible®, Copyright © 1960, 1971 by The Lockman Foundation. Used by permission. All rights reserved. Lockman.org.

Scripture marked (NJKV) taken from the New King James Version®. Copyright © 1982 by Thomas Nelson. Used by permission. All rights reserved.

Paperback ISBN: 979-8-9899945-0-2
Hardcover ISBN: 979-8-9899945-1-9
E-book ISBN: 979-8-9899945-2-6

Library of Congress Control Number: 2024908436

Printed in the United States of America

Disclaimer: These true stories are seen as factual through the eyes of the one who lived and chronicled them, so are based on the author's experiences and opinions, expounded by his personal interpretations, and wide open to others good will observations. However, before we deliberate in love, dear one, it is wise to remember that a man with an experience is rarely at the mercy of a man with an argument. Maybe never here. Names and places may have been altered to protect the innocent.

Dedication

To Holy Spirit, without whom we can do nothing (John 15:5b).

To my Proverbs 31 wife, Emily, without whose love, over twenty years of encouragement, patience, and support this work would still be the stuff of dreams (Prov. 18:22).

To each soul kissed by Heaven as a participant in this book, who returned to give God the glory due His name (1 John 4:19, Matt. 10:8b).

Contents

Acknowledgments

Commander Pritchard, USN, a squared-away Marine lance corporal, Marine Major Cooney, Air Force Col. Dick and Nurse Darlene, and Pastor Mac Wright, Stephen and Gerry, Melanie and John Woodworth, Dr. Frank Turner, MD, Northwest Medical Teams, World Vision International, and an elderly Baptist missionary, a desperate young man from Tulsa, Robert Curry's team of evangelists, a Tennessee evangelist and a little mute girl, Rev. Milford Kirkpatrick, Pastor Bob and expatriate George, "Jesse Vesuvius," an Irish lass, Lonnie Noblet and Addison Woodworth, Vietnamese children with fresh smiles, "Paul" (an Oregon logger), Mike and Lori Salley (Show Mercy International), the street people on a Texas Christmas, Pastor Hubert Robert Curry, many warring, guardian, and messenger angels, Beth Lottig, and Gary Jeter, computer scribe and friend. Thanks for participating in this effort to bring Father glory due His name. For those "Flown West" (airmen's lingo for having passed), be certain to give our love to Jesus and our Father in Heaven.

A Note from Coauthor Emily

Living a life of "Kisses from Heaven" has been an adventure as the wife of a man who is obedient to the call of God day or night, rain or shine, snow or sleet . . . you understand. My husband is a true servant of the Lord.

When we started this journey twenty-six years ago by marrying, leaving our jobs, selling our home, and moving into a small motorhome, it was, admittedly, a stretch for me. But what a marvelous stretch it became because we dared to lay down the things of this world, pick up the cross of Christ, and follow hard after Him.

We quickly became acutely aware of God's voice and unspoken interactions with us as we continued to diligently seek and—soon, it seemed—find Him everywhere we turned. Then, every glorious adventure would be followed by another.

As you read this book, keep in mind a lifestyle like this can be a tad unpredictable, if not chaotic, to say the least; although it has not always been easy, it has absolutely been fulfilling. Whether or not you choose to follow a path like ours, know that God is always with us, always speaking and forever working. It is simply up to us to make a conscious effort to make ourselves available and aware of His purposefully laboring in our lives and the lives of those around us.

If we seek Him with all our hearts, He will soon be found, and all because he helped us get out of our own ways to make room for His.

Preface

"I would have despaired unless I had believed that I would
see the goodness of the Lord in the land of the living."
—Psalm 27:13

Following the wedding at Cana, where Jesus reluctantly changed 720 quarts of fresh water into fine wine, His disciples' belief in Him was secured (John 2:11). Thereafter, the multitudes began following Him not so much for His well-received gospel (John 7:46) as for the way He gave it teeth with more miracles (Matt. 9:33). Soon, the Lord faced the necessity to prove His gospel to the contemptuous pharisees, scribes, and other doubters. Healing the paralytic lowered through His roof by four friends was one strategy. "Which is easier, to say, 'Your sins have been forgiven you,'" Jesus questioned the ridiculing religious leaders, "or to say, 'Rise and walk'? But in order that you may know that the Son of Man has authority on Earth to forgive sins," He said to the paralytic, "I say to you, rise, and take up your stretcher and go home" (Luke 5:23–24). The man promptly did while all in attendance—including those pharisees and scribes present, we are told—were astonished and glorified God. To no surprise, Jesus shortly came to this public admonition of truth: "Unless you *people* see signs and wonders, you *simply* will not believe" (John 4:48).

Since then, people have changed no more than Jesus, who the Bible states is the same yesterday, today, and forever (Heb. 13:8). From Thomas the Doubter needing to touch the Lord's wounds to believe

(John 20:27) to the elderly grandma's ultimatum of "Where's the Beef?" in the classic Wendy's commercial, we see humankind's need to see proof before committing to nearly any earthly undertaking. So Jesus chose not to profess He was Messiah when John the Baptist sent his disciples to ask if He was the One . . . "or do we look for someone else?" (Luke 7:20). Instead, the Lord instructed them to simply let John know of His miraculous works to identify Him (Luke 7:23) as Messiah.

Understandably, before ascending to the Father, the Lord did not alter His unchangeable gospel but, instead, not only left us capable of His wonderous works but also "greater works" to defend it (John 14:12); then He promised us a Helper (Holy Spirit) to guarantee that would happen (Acts 1:8). Why? Perhaps the Lord knew we would need more miraculous help to convince others of His gospel during our ungodly days than during His.

So what is a miracle? The Merriam-Webster Dictionary defines a miracle as an extraordinary event manifesting divine intervention in human affairs. Take a moment to digest how this long-accepted characterization embraces a potentially broad and "greater than" spectrum of differences, numbers, and varieties of extraordinary divine interventions in our daily lives while always involving and depending upon Holy Spirit to bring them about. "Apart from Me," Jesus said, "you can do nothing" (John 15:5b).

What you are about to read, if we haven't lost you, are excerpts from the blessed life of an everyday Christian, a native-born, tax-paying, patriotic American, Naval aviator, Vietnam veteran, medical doctor, pastor, long-term/short-term missionary, and restoration (i.e., inner healing) minister. Along with my co-laborer, intercessor wife, Emily, I've found that Jesus loves to weave His miraculous ways (unique, inexplicable, extraordinary, supernatural exploits) often incognito, always purposefully—and frequently in the eleventh hour—through the lives of believers to encourage them and convince unbelievers of

His gospel. "Freely you received, freely give" (Matt. 10:8) has always been the way of our others-centered Savior (Luke 6:38).

(You will forgive us if our tales are somewhat more modest than the Lord's.)

The Lord asked us in 2002 to chronicle His God Stories from our lives and pay them forward to the body of Christ and those looking for proof. These God Stories aim to show the following: Jesus is alive and well on planet Earth (Heb. 13:8), His gospel is true today as ever (John 17:17), He still works to eagerly offer His salvation, gifts of the Holy Spirit germane to present times, and a divine, intimate, and relevant personal relationship with Him is available for all who believe (Eph. 2:8). All the above, you might note, are "greater than" works.

Consider these thoughts: While the Lord's world was replete with the blind, deaf, lame, lepers, and demon-possessed, Jesus convinced the multitudes He was the Messiah and His gospel was true by addressing such contemporary issues as healing the sick and delivering the demonized. With today's increased availability of modern medical and psychiatric care to address a vast number of those age-old burdens, there appears to be a shifting of our interest to a potpourri of spiritual events. In this modern day, we look to additional miracles, such as unique near-death experiences (NDEs); inexplicable rescues from impending tragedy; extraordinary resurrections of relationships or deliverances from addictions to drugs, alcohol, sexual perversion, and the underworld; supernatural encounters with angels or His divine presence; or unexpected blessings arriving with no way to legitimately explain them but a supernatural Jesus.

Briefly, the proof contemporary humanity requires to believe in Jesus as Lord and His gospel true are unique, inexplicable, extraordinary, or supernatural experiences with no explanation outside God's personal care and intervention to explain their origin.

Let us whet your appetite for this little book of God's Stories with the following mini Kiss from Heaven and testimony of God's abundant concern for the everyday travails and delights of His children. Will you see this God Story as coincidence, good karma, kismet, luck, or chance—all anathemas in the life of a Christian where God orders every step (Ps. 37:23–24)? Or will you see it as an up-close-and-personal encounter choreographed by our loving Savior intervening in the affairs of His children with a miracle attesting to who He is and what He loves to do in our lives?

A Kiss from Heaven

Can you believe that a young woman abandoned by, estranged from, and incommunicado with her biological father for an entire twenty-year span was living a life so filled with hurt, anger, bitterness, and hatred toward him that in desperation she finally sought help from her prison of unforgiveness? Of course you can.

Can you believe that by the end of her ministry session with Holy Spirit (well, we were there, too), she had confessed her many sins of anger, repented, found forgiveness, His truth to set her free, healing from her pain and then, instantly, experienced a fervent longing to reconcile with her father after long years of hate and discontent? Harder? Sure.

Can you believe that twenty minutes after Emily and I left her home came a knock on the young woman's door, where her father stood asking for forgiveness and pleading for a fresh start with the daughter lost to him for two decades?

No? Then you do not know our eleventh-hour Jesus (Ps. 37:23–24).

Yes? Then read on, saint, and discover the Lord is impartial, plays no favorites, and is no respecter of persons (Acts 10:34). He is ready and willing to prepare you for your own "Kisses from Heaven" God's Stories—believable and contemporary testimonies to bring Jesus to life in both yours and others' worlds as Savior and Lord.

If meaningful encounters brought the lost to Jesus in His time, shouldn't they do the same today? All we need do is believe, learn to wait patiently while about our busy days, become alert listeners amid their noise, and—when Holy Spirit divinely interrupts and prompts us in our secret places—hear Him instantly, heed Him joyfully, and obey Him completely.

Then, when wondrous "Kisses from Heaven" follow as God's Stories testifying to the goodness of God in the land of the living (Ps. 27:13), remember to pay them forward. Why? Simple: They are not our stories, Christian; they are the Lord's. So freely receive and freely give. Then, when God's love stories begin to purposefully flow from your life to the afflicted and needy, watch for hard hearts to soften, stiff necks to turn, prodigals to return, and His chosen to come home to Jesus.

Introduction (2023)

This is a book of God Stories. That bold statement demands explanation. Who speaks for God? Not this man. So let's try to define a God Story not by its content—for as we will see, each story speaks for itself—but by what criteria qualifies it to bear such a heady title. Is there a higher experience for a born-again Christian than to become a privileged moving part in a wonderous story created, choreographed, and christened by the Father, the only One who can guarantee Himself the glory He deserves? Let us see what it takes, at least from the eyes of this mere human.

God's Intimate Presence

God's intimate involvement defines a God Story. Remove Father's hand, and there is no story, at least not one worth telling. Test that statement; read a God Story. Then, remove all the elements that make it unique, inexplicable, extraordinary, or supernatural. The result? The story ends! It becomes an unfinished event, inconclusive and void of any meaning on Earth or glowing significance in Heaven. A God Story excluding God becomes a hollow collection of thoughts, words, and actions, a narrative with no divine worth or purpose.

God's Wondrous Character

A God Story always portrays the character and works of God as wonderous. What has happened in the story makes it difficult to describe or discuss without reaching beyond the ordinary and into the sublime. Applying uncertain or ill-defined words like luck, kismet, karma, serendipity, coincidence, or chance to explain a God Story only tarnishes the story's credibility and diminishes its meaning. Father's thumbprints, often hidden throughout a tale, are enough to confirm its place as a God Story.

God's Benevolent Intent

God Stories are uplifting, encouraging, edifying, or comforting for both those participating in the story and those listening to it further on as a testimony. God Stories leave no doubt as to Father's pristine character (proving who He is) and His infinite power (displaying what He does). Even more, they reinforce His loving intent toward us, which always supplies listeners with grateful hearts, elevated faith, and awe, if not worship for His inalterably benevolent heart and beneficent ways.

God's Lifelong Lessons

Lessons well learned remain as jewels mined from the residual of any passing God Story. Whether with knowledge gained relevant to a specific moment or wisdom applicable to life over the long haul, the Lord rarely transits our lives without teaching His tailored truth. All we need to do is slow down and allow Holy Spirit to unwrap the truth waiting for us in any God Story, whether arising from our own or others' testimonies.

God's Glory Due His Name

A God Story preeminently exalts God for who He is, what He does, and only by way of a moment He deems worthy of His glory. So what greater privilege for a Christian than to be invited to play a living role in a God Story, where He is at His glorified best, and the unabashed purpose is to bring Him the glory due His name? Then the God Story becomes an inevitable unsolicited Kiss from Heaven for any believer taking a privileged part, and, finally, brings an unchangeable living testimony of God's majesty even to those of us participating vicariously.

Questions

Do you question God's desire to bring you a story for His glory? How can you be certain that you are ready to hear Him? Are you a waiter and listener with ears necessary to hear? Are you ready to obey instantly, joyfully, and completely when you do?[1] Are you ready for God to intervene in your most mundane of daily events or in the middle of the most impossibly demanding and inconvenient of situations? Are you willing to drop everything at a moment's notice to have your life turned upside down by God interrupting you in the most uncomfortable, inflexible, or humiliating of ways?

Are you then willing to deny yourself, pick up your cross, and follow Him? Are you willing to lay down your life for your friend? Are you willing to enter an inferno for making your decision to accompany Him at all costs? How about bearing accusations of irresponsibility for not being a Christian, being a Christian in name only, a sociopathic liar, a hyper-spiritual whacko, unhinged, or demon-possessed? Ready to lose friends? Good friends? Family? Close family? Church family? Face jealousy? Condemnation? Rejection? Abandonment? Persecution?

We need not go further, do we? But we could. And Jesus did. So if you are not ready to follow Him down this narrow highway, faithfully keep doing what you are doing that pleases Him. Though all

---

[1] Joy Dawson, *Forever Ruined for the Ordinary* (Edinburgh, Scotland: Thomas Nelson, 2001).

His highways are narrow, and but one leads to the Father, there are many paths through His kingdom. If you are ready for a wilderness journey into another promised land of milk and honey, adventurous "Caleb," let Him know, be on the alert, and keep your toothbrush on call and your backpack packed. Then, prepare yourself for the most remarkable years of your life. Always be aware—God is impartial, no respecter of persons, and more than ready to deliver you a Kiss from Heaven as an arrow in your evangelical quiver as a testimony to His glory.

Postscript

Throughout this tome's writings, you will come across dependable "Postscripts" designed to give Holy Spirit a chance to comment or the author (more often scribe) to enter his ten cents' worth. When occasional lighthearted tales may seem to fall outside the parameters of a God Story, I admit to adding such delights only after consideration, which you, too, may deem adequate as a Kiss from Heaven.

Nevertheless, please honor these tales as God-given (meaning they are purposeful) and Heaven-sent to serve as testimonies 1) to the goodness of God in the land of the living (Ps. 27:13), 2) to enable Jesus, both His gospel and His words, to become relative to our times and believable as lights to a progressively darkening world, and 3) to equip individual Christians to carry unique, inexplicable, extraordinary, and supernatural testimonies to build faith for themselves, convince others of His presence, and prove the gospel as apostasy grows, churches close, and our Bible is outlawed.

No one participating in a God Story will ever be the same. They will commonly be ruined for the ordinary but equipped with a living testimony to build their own faith, draw others to Christ, and bring glory to Father. I must ask, Christian, when our race is run, "Have we any greater reason for inhabiting God's green Earth?"

Outskirts of Heaven (1974)

S cattered throughout North San Diego County during the decade of the 1970s were isolated pockets of vigorous residential growth, which, unknown to us, were the heralds of Southern California's upcoming building craze. Like unwary victims in the path of a colossus tornado, countless ancient orange and avocado groves, backyard horse farms, ranches, ranchettes, and little hamlets that had long endeared themselves to their small-town-minded communities were all too soon swallowed by the insatiable vortex of California's new burgeoning home construction Goliath.

The 300-acre Daley Ranch—for generations home to thousands of contented cattle leisurely grazing away their undemanding lives beneath the California sun by day and packs of yelping coyotes running down their fashionably late moonlit dinners by night—was smack dab in Goliath's path with no David in sight. The ranch, slumbering among picturesque boulder-strewn mountains crisscrossed by a myriad of trails winding their way through seas of lush green and scented wild lilacs, was home to Hilltop Circle, an inaptly named perfect square of roadway carved out years before from the vast Daley empire, and was now home to a couple of dozen families clinging to their little pieces of Heaven on Earth.

Driving Miss Daisy Crazy

North of the Circle by a few miles was a not-so-vigorous pocket of residential growth, the smallish senior community of Rancho Bernardo, slow moving enough to crown it the town where folks drove as if every road bisected a school zone. That may sound amusing, quaint, and even heartwarming, but it was not. Did this explain all the pokey traffic in that little village? Hardly. It was not until uninitiated drivers understood that senior citizens using turn signals at intersections were rarely committed to their choices—or octogenarians seemingly stalled at four-way stop signs were merely catnapping—that the genesis of the town's traffic creep became progressively clearer. The whole problem, you see, began so innocently.

It was easy to commend the concern arising in the hearts of drivers yet unaware of Rancho Bernardo's little traffic idiosyncrasies. The uninitiated who came upon an intersection where a stationary vehicle with a solitary blinking directional signal held a slumped-over senior citizen at the wheel gave more than ample reason to pull over to lend a hand. But do not be deceived, friend. Newton was right: Every action has an equal and opposite reaction. How so? Well, we now had not one but two automobiles blocking the entrance to a busy four-way intersection—with more to come, I might add. To hardened veteran Rancho Bernardo road warriors, such scenes struck concern of another kind.

History had taught us the uncertainty of what was prone to happen next. Only those in the know understood that the old man behind that wheel was rarely dead, as the approaching Good Samaritans had assumed, but ready to rise as a Phoenix from the ashes of his REM reverie, a somnambulant, confused, and directionally challenged Rip Van Winkle—foot on a roaring accelerator and ready to ride the four-wheeled, two-ton missile he commanded like the reincarnation of Dr. Strangelove's bomb.

No one knew, least of all the old guy, which of the four cardinal directions would have the privilege of accommodating that four-wheeled projectile.

So the first domino fell when the old boy, startled by his own awakening and the exploding horns of the nasty traffic jam he had singlehandedly created, rammed his unsuspecting Betsy into gear to roar off like a funny car at the nationals. Try and visualize the panic as fellow drivers—trapped four deep at four different four-way stop signs—in mass unison enforced last-ditch efforts to seek safety through squealing U-turns, futile escapes down vacated driveways, and across manicured lawns—some passing one another on the shoulders of two-lane roads while inadvertently spewing mailboxes like sunflower seeds from a coach's Friday night pie hole, and others, in desperation, abandoning their vehicles and diving for the inside comfort of roadside culverts or joining the Zacchaeus family in the nearest Sycamore tree of which, praise Jesus, San Diego had transplanted a plethora from Australia—or were those Eucalyptus? It makes minor difference, friend; it was the Egyptian army fleeing the Sinai all over again during the six-day war, which, only because of rich volumes of experience, took three to four minutes in Rancho Bernardo. Being prone toward literary license here may muddle the facts but also helps us to grasp why traffic occasionally got a little pokey in Rancho Bernardo during the 1970s. Most citizens would have agreed, despite my overstatement, that to live in this sleepy little village required them to develop a solid knack for defensive driving while buying a generous-sized State Farm umbrella policy merely to prepare for the inevitable.

Okay, now to the serious stuff.

New Friends at Pomerado

For those who valiantly survived Sunday morning's traffic creep, the services were always noteworthy at Pomerado Christian Church, found a stone's throw from the center of sleepy little Rancho Bernardo. It was not so much Brother Mac Wright's down-home preaching as it was his honest way of following Jesus and loving others that always refreshed and encouraged me to press on into the next week's killer schedule as a resident physician at the Balboa Naval Hospital in San Diego. Completing one Sunday service, Mac took me by the arm and led us to a couple of first-time visitors standing in our church's narthex. Dick, ramrod straight and movie star handsome, was a recently retired Air Force colonel and F-105 Thunderchief driver fresh from the skies over Hanoi, while Darlene, his equally stunning wife, was a registered nurse, now retired. Dick had long looked forward to completing his career as a military aviator to enter civilian life. Darlene, diagnosed with terminal metastatic cancer, could only look forward to entering Heaven. As a former Marine aviator, I easily bonded with Dick and, as a medical professional, Darlene.

Weeks stretched into months. Dick looked as if his new way of life was agreeing with him; Darlene increasingly appeared as if she were seeking the open arms of Jesus. It seemed so disheartening—just when this couple might have been adventuring into the shared autumn of their lives, they were about to go their separate ways. Then, within weeks, Dick and Darlene could no longer attend church services together. Shortly, in the capable hands of hospice, Darlene was spending her days in a hospital bed crowded into the center of their neat, if now shrunken, living room. Finally, there was little for me but to encourage and pray while watching helplessly as her enemy within won battle after battle.

A Divine Intercept

Pushing past 2:00 a.m. after multiple trips to the cast room to manage a few fractures, admitting a fistful of patients for the next day's surgeries, and managing a zillion phone calls, I had completed my night's work at the Balboa Naval Hospital. Or so I thought.

There was but one thing on my mind: sleep! Wasting no time on my way to the physicians' call room while computing the number of "zzzzz's" that could be milked out of the next four short hours before morning rounds, Jesus spoke to my spirit: "Go to the fourth floor."

I well knew our service had no patients on that floor, so I reminded the Lord, "Lord, we have no patients on the fourth floor."

Jesus repeated Himself: "Go to the fourth floor!"

Repeating myself, as if the Lord had not been listening, let me only hope to never hear Him speak again with the emphasis that followed. Quickly doing an about-face, I climbed one flight of stairs to, you guessed it, the fourth floor where our service had no patients. To our right, after exiting the stairwell, was the pediatric ward divided down the center by a large partition lined on each side by an estimated thirty beds. Opposite each bed and pressed against each outside wall of the cavernous room were an added thirty companion beds. The sole light in that enormous ward came from the nurse's station adjacent to the entrance. The far recess of the space was like peering into a coal mine at midnight. Barely taking time to survey the scene, I whispered confidently, "See, Lord, we have no patients on the fourth floor."

That, I thought, should take care of that. Poised to head directly to the call room, my curiosity piqued; what was that indistinct form lurking in the twilight bordering the far reaches of that coal mine? Inquisitive, I hurried directly to the dimly lit area. In its deepening shadows, one adult hovered over another, lying in an undersized pediatric bed. This couple? Dick and Darlene. "What are you doing here?" I whispered.

Dick explained quietly, "When her condition worsened tonight, I tried to call your home with no luck. So I phoned the hospital and was assigned to the only beds available, which were in pediatrics." The concern and fatigue etched in his eyes were for a good reason: Darlene was about to leave us. Slipping past Dick to the head of the little bed where his wife was taking her final breath, we saw Darlene begin her journey to Jesus. Dick knew, and with tears in our eyes, we prayed. Letting him know that I would take care of the death certificate and call the mortician, Dick went along.

It was 5:25 a.m. when I completed the paperwork and phone calls. That meant thirty-five minutes before morning rounds. Aching fatigue pulsated through my entire body while racing down the stairwell to the third-floor corridor leading to relief. "Fifteen minutes," I pled wishfully, "if I can steal but fifteen minutes." Opening the call room door, I jettisoned myself upon the bed.

An Unexpected Journey

There was no time for surprise or confusion. My exhausted head had not burrowed into the waiting overstuffed hospital pillow for more than a millisecond before a scene, more real than life itself, burst forth around me. Alone on a lush green cushion of green grass, I overlooked a peaceful wide-blue river. The day was exquisite and crowned by a powder blue sky showing off a smattering of puffy fair-weather clouds. A soothing breeze massaged my cheeks, mitigating the heat of a noonday sun. A bee buzzed in the distance. Across the water's divide, there were three verdant, rolling mountains linked arm in arm, each one ablaze with countless wildflowers of every conceivable color and hue and more distinct and brilliant than possible in our world. Before I could apprehend that beauty, an invisible hand snatched me from the riverbank; then, suspended mere inches off the water, it carried me toward the far side of the river. As if sighting through a zoom lens or skimming the water in a fast-moving helicopter, within heartbeats, I leapt the far bank, flashed over a flower-studded meadow, and was now accelerating up one of those brightly decorated mountains.

Climbing at breakneck speed, a human form appeared far ahead, making its way upward. Closing quickly and within seconds, that form took the shape of a woman clothed in a pale-yellow taffeta dress and wearing a matching wide-brimmed summer sombrero. As the final distance collapsed and ended between us, she, at that precise instant, glanced over her right shoulder and smiled. It was Darlene.

As prompt as my arrival on this breathtaking scene was my return to the call room's bed. Glancing at my watch, it had been mere seconds. Somehow, I knew without question that Holy Spirit and I had invaded the outskirts of Heaven; just over those flower-strewn mountains, I felt certain, was the dwelling place of our eternal King. And praise the Lord, by now, Darlene would be on final approach. A flood of peace overtook me and left me unbelievably refreshed. Rolling out of bed, I cleaned up and headed, with ample time to spare, to morning rounds and a brand-new glorious day with Jesus.

An Unexpected Lesson

At the pastor's request, I took the pulpit at Darlene's memorial service days later. Gazing for a moment at the gathering of quiet, respectful faces before relaying my still-fresh call room experience following her passing, my testimony surfaced deeply powerful emotions that, despite my effort to control them, colored that vivid narrative. Intent on comforting and encouraging Dick and the entire congregation with what the Lord had revealed during that Heavenly outer vision, as the saga unfolded before these people who loved me as a brother Christian, trusted physician, and devoted father, I unexpectedly saw a metamorphosis of many faces.

Gradually changing from a sea of calm reverence into a Pandora's Box of outwardly mixed expressions, there were those weeping, others praising, and those smiling while nodding with assurance. Still others stared directly ahead, lost in withdrawal or confusion. Then there were the frozen, confused as if challenged by an invisible threat. Isolated folks seemed angry, even hostile, and ready to either confront or flee a sudden repugnant situation. Stunned and puzzled that somehow my testimony had ushered in an emotional cloud to hover over Darlene's and Dick's dear friends and family members was distressing. When the service was complete, the congregation greeted me, some more cordially than others, with only a handful mentioning the presentation. From that moment on, I sensed, with sadness of spirit, that my place in the hearts of my dear friends in that body of believers had changed and not for the good.

Years later, I came to understand what happened that day; I had inadvertently crossed the Rubicon of Western Christianity, and, for a handful in this church family, it was my river of no return. Unwittingly, I had publicly resurrected and confirmed otherworldly reality as an integral part of the American Christian experience by testifying to the intentional, close, personal, and tangible involvement of the miraculous in the lives of today's church. To a handful, I had committed an "unpardonable" sin by tainting the clear doctrines of men with the muddy waters of a supernatural witness.

The encounter with Holy Spirit had shaken my roots, the roots of my church, and my place among that lovely little body of believers, which, sadly, would never be the same. This, I eventually realized, was often the predictable outcome whenever a saint is trapped in the struggle between flesh and Spirit.

Postscript

Remember the now world-famous byline by the late radio news commentator Paul Harvey, "And now, the rest of the story"? Arranging for personal end-of-life care for Darlene and providing Dick a ready medical resource within the local body revealed Father's compassionate concern for this couple's difficult last days while orchestrating the time of her death with my call night added even more love. Still, the Lord was unfinished. He was about to move into His arena of faith.

Although my outer vision (trance) blessed Dick and others, that testimony had a far different impact when it caused a small group of saints in the local body to stumble. Do not let this alarm or dismay you when this happens. Tales of supernatural moments often divide flesh

8

from Spirit, building faith in those who have experienced them but fear and doubt in those who have not. Listen to Thomas the Doubter: "Unless I shall see in His hands the imprint of the nails . . . and put my hand into His side, I will not believe" (John 20:25). Now, by that time, all the remaining disciples had met the resurrected Jesus and believed, while Thomas had done neither. Personal experience augments faith. Jesus knew that and said to Thomas, "Reach here your hand, and put it into My side; and be not unbelieving but believing." Thomas, doing so, answered and said to him, "My Lord and my God!" (John 20:27–28). That experience settled the conflict, didn't it?

Dear one, a man armed with an experience is never at the mercy of one with an argument. If you have had a supernatural encounter, no one can convince you otherwise. Then, as you believe, you will open the door for another such experience. Christian, if you have not had a supernatural experience, as Thomas had with Jesus, you may be a doubter until you do. So challenge the Lord with prayer. Didn't Jesus say, "Until now you have asked for nothing in My name; ask, and you will receive, that your joy may be made full" (John 16:24)? Then, get ready to enjoy the faithfulness of God to His Word, and be expecting your own glorious Kiss from Heaven.

QUESTION: Where is the Kiss from Heaven in this God Story?

ANSWER: I had never experienced such an extraordinary divine intervention as the merciful management of our dear couple's difficult plight that night. Have you? Then, how about the Lord opening my eyes to the "other side," beginning with a definitive inner conversation with Jesus and ending with a truer-than-life outer vision (trance) portraying our sister Darlene trekking through the outskirts of Heaven. As a finale came her "back to Earth" memorial service, opening the eyes of my heart to a deeper understanding of the Church's complex and profoundly diverse—and sometimes divisive—ingrained responses to otherworldly events . . . which, of course, I have eventually but sadly come to not understand at all.

♥ 2

Outskirts of Heaven (2005)

G erry and Stephen were dear friends. We fellowshipped together for three years at the turn of the century as winter Texans at Long Island Village, a heavily senior RV park in Port Isabel on the very tip of Texas, two short miles across the Queen Isabella causeway from South Padre Island. Have I got you located? Besides participating in a home group together, we attended the same body of believers and genuinely enjoyed each other's company. Then Gerry became ill. Stephen described her illness as a protracted common cold, at least until she had difficulty swallowing. So he called me one evening, and I headed for a look.

Gerry had some pharyngeal edema, a swelling in her throat, presumed secondary to an unknown allergen or infection causing her distress. She was mildly uncomfortable and in no grave distress, so I gave her an OTC (over-the-counter) antihistamine to help mitigate any potential airway problems before we left for the hospital emergency room forty minutes away for more definitive examination and therapy. An emergency medicine physician supported the diagnosis, although by now the earlier medication had made Gerry rest much easier. He then gave her an intramuscular injection of steroid and discharged her from care.

The three of us left the hospital around midnight, settled into

Stephen's big four-door truck, and set sail for home. Holy Spirit suggested I share with Gerry about the time He took me to the outskirts of Heaven. "Lord," I argued silently, "that trip was thirty years ago, Gerry is sick, and we are all tired."

"Tell her the story," He firmly urged. Wisely, I resisted Him no further.

"Gerry," I asked, rotating toward the back seat where she was quietly curled, "would you like to hear about my trip to the outskirts of Heaven?" She was all for it; so I began the account, detailing the entire journey. Winding up the story, she kindly thanked me. It was not long before Stephen pulled into their driveway.

Here We Go Again

The next morning, I contacted Stephen only to discover that Gerry's symptoms had recurred in spades. He called the paramedics and was about to follow the ambulance to the hospital; my car was in his wake. Stephen and I were chatting in an ER bay, waiting for Gerry to return from the CT scanner. Upon her return, she complained of difficulty moving her lower extremities. Included in the on-call neurologist's presumptive diagnoses was Guillain-Barré syndrome (GBS), a debilitating, ascending, and often lengthy paralysis attributed at the time to many causes and years later as an infamous complication of the swine flu (2009) and more recently Covid (2019). This diagnosis often leads to protracted years of treatment, rehabilitation, and slow but uncertain recovery. This was not good news at all and led to immediate concern over the uncertainty Gerry faced.

That dreaded ascending progressive paralysis rapidly reached her chest muscles and diminished her ability to talk and, shortly, to breathe on her own. The physicians present abandoned their discussion and called stat for an anesthesiologist, who immediately intubated Gerry and placed her on a ventilator. Within moments, the doctor administered sedation as Gerry's gurney left for the medical floor to start plasmapheresis, a method to filter the blood plasma of proteins incriminated in Guillain-Barré syndrome.

Unknown to Gerry or Stephen, she had begun, as noted earlier, what physicians would foresee as a difficult struggle from months to years of total body paralysis to an unpredictable level of recovery. Those treating her would have counseled her as much that day had they not been so busy saving her life. When I followed Gerry to the floor after her admission, the paralysis had stolen control of her body, save her eyelids. As a prisoner to this dread condition, she was aware of everything about her, felt each uncomfortable wrinkle from her bedsheets, every itch that begged for a scratch, and all the probing, poking, and testing that goes on hour after hour in any hospital setting. Regrettably, she could not speak or do anything to alleviate the discomfort. So, immobile and powerless to respond to this nightmare in any way, Gerry lay helpless and, I confidently presumed, terror-ridden.

The medical community responded by being "realistic," while Stephen and Gerry, we discovered later, were, instead, exercising their faith in prayer. As a Christian physician, scenarios like this had always been muddy. After thirty-plus years, I had seen enough of these diagnoses that the rarely predictable severity and unknown long-term prognoses left unsettled questions with respect to Gerry. Coming to mind was a case published in a medical journal years before about a woman who did not recover from her Guillain-Barré paralysis for over thirty-six grueling months, only to spend years thereafter trying to regain her strength. Admittedly programmed by my "great learning" (Acts 26:24), still, I had seen the Lord miraculously heal a variety of conditions on the mission field, occasionally using my own hands. There was an inner conflict; I cannot deny it. That conflict would not last long.

Three days later, Gerry was moving her toes, and within two more days, she had experienced full return of function to her diaphragm and respiratory muscles, was extubated off the ventilator, could speak, and was able to take nourishment by mouth. By the seventh day, she was walking without assistance and on the way home. The treating physicians had readily acknowledged the short duration of her case as unprecedented at the time; one doctor even used the word "miracle." According to every professional involved in Gerry's care, the medical literature had no recorded cases of Guillain-Barré syndrome with such a rapid recovery. Jesus occasionally ignores the medical literature, if you haven't noticed.

Now, the Rest of the Story

Emily and I were about to return to our family home in Upstate New York. We were both exhausted; it had been a taxing week spent gathering and squeezing our belongings into a far too small U-Haul trailer. On the way out of town, I opted to call Stephen and Gerry, with whom we had not spoken since her recent discharge from the hospital. While we were bidding a fond farewell to Stephen, Gerry was cooking dinner, and, except for the minimal unsteadiness her husband reported, she was like new. Asking if I had a moment to talk, Gerry took the phone and shared the following remarkable story.

Petrified beyond description upon that emergency department gurney, the movement of her legs rapidly progressed from weakness to full paralysis. Then, within minutes, the paralysis raced to her abdomen, chest, and neck. Barely able to breathe or swallow, Gerry soon found her entire voluntary muscle system incapacitated despite her greatest effort to move. Under the grip of this terrifying state and unable to breathe, she was losing consciousness when a physician inserted an endotracheal tube and attached it to what she knew was a ventilator. Now, at least she would not die of asphyxia, a fear which had overtaken her until that very moment.

Taken to the medical floor where doctors, nurses, and specialty support personnel raced purposefully about her room over the next few hours, Gerry's hectic day, without warning, ended at a snail's pace. Room emptied of medical help, she found herself alone in the darkness with her only companions the rhythmic sounds of her ventilator, the aggravating beeping of unattended alarms, and the distant intermittent voices wafting into her room from somewhere down distant corridors.

The whirlwind had ended, and in the relative calm of her now darkened room, Gerry experienced a rapidly growing sense of terror, which quickly escalated into sheer panic. She was alone, vulnerable, and had no one to help. Then, without warning, a figurative firestorm swept over her body, consuming her with excruciating pain. In desperation and having no other recourse, Gerry cried out to the Lord, not in the silence of her room but in the chaos of her mind: "Jesus, I cannot go on with this unbearable pain and burning; I am so alone and afraid. What is happening to me?"

Somewhere during her frantic prayer, Gerry pled, "Lord, help me; please take me to the cool meadow covered with green grass and wildflowers that Doctor Woodworth shared on our way home from the hospital last night." In a heartbeat, Gerry found herself in that same lush, beautiful meadow, her body nestled in a cushion of refreshing cool grass perfumed with the scent of countless wildflowers at the base of that color-drenched mountain. Then, bathed in what she knew was the calming presence of Jesus, her fear melted away while, simultaneously, the overwhelming agony of burning stopped. Suddenly, Gerry was comfortable, pain-free, and unafraid.

For the next seventy-two hours, she rested in the total peace of her meadow, even when hospital workers, tending to their assigned duties, disturbed her. After three days, when Gerry realized that the Lord was answering her prayers for healing, she left her place of comfort in the meadow and "returned" to her hospital room to face a daily routine. Four days later, Gerry was home cooking dinner for Stephen.

Postscript

Admittedly, I had rarely, if ever, shared my trip to the outskirts of Heaven with anyone before that night with Gerry. The opportunity had never presented itself at a suitable moment when the story would have glorified God and blessed others, not seemed self-aggrandizing, or made me appear a lunatic, liar, or demonically oppressed. That little vignette, nearly forgotten over the years, had been maturing quietly in the wine cellar of Father's heart. Aged to perfection, He offered it to Gerry at the precise moment to fill her upcoming yet unrecognized need. Can you see how Jesus never gives blessings for us to hoard but to liberally pass on in His perfect timing? "Freely you received," says the Master, "freely give" (Matt. 10:8). Don't we all need to do better?

As it was with Jesus's teachings and parables, Gerry's Kiss from Heaven—and each of our own—have similar purposes. Those would primarily be to draw folks to Jesus, build their faith, and glorify Father in Heaven. From her discharge from the hospital, Gerry's blessing has been to share her testimony from an unscheduled, all-expense-paid, three-day vacation to a lush, multicolored meadow on the outskirts of Heaven where the Lord was her shepherd, she did not want, He made her to lie down in green pastures, He led her beside still waters, and He restored her soul (Ps. 23:1–3). Oh, forget not her body.

And, if you have not noticed, dear Christian, Gerry, by proxy, has once again shared that amazing Kiss from Heaven with us.

QUESTION: Where is the Kiss from Heaven from this God Story?

ANSWER: It had always seemed odd that the God Story Holy Spirit gave Gerry from my past laid dormant for so many years. But because time is always in the present for God, that Kiss from Heaven from years past became fresh manna for Gerry. The supernatural haven of rest in my vision provided a place of perfect peace for her to experience an extraordinary increased rate of healing (i.e., in the presence of Jesus, her healer), recognized as a miracle by at least one physician, Gerry, Stephen, and a whole lot of Christian friends looking on. Didn't Gerry's testimony, built upon my own, add a convincing evangelical arrow and Kiss from Heaven to our blessed friend's quiver to bring glory to Father?

Outskirts of Heaven (2009)

S tephen felt puny over the weeks preceding his illness in South Texas, so he stopped playing his morning game of tennis, which troubled everyone. Of equal concern was his decision to wait until his return to Green Bay to see a doctor. When he did, the news was not good. Then, complications with his coronary artery bypass surgery left him holding on to life by a thread but wishing the Lord would cut it quickly and schedule him a trip to Heaven. He got his wish, and soon Gerry found herself alone in their big country home, which she could not keep up due to the few residuals of the Guillain-Barré syndrome. So she moved to a nice first-floor apartment in town, and, after a time, the Lord supplied a sweet young nurse, who lived a floor above, as a friend to run errands and otherwise help when necessary.

Understandably, Gerry was lonely and felt a deep sadness. Oh, she was confident that Stephen was in Heaven and that it would be merely a matter of time before she would see him again. Still, that was little consolation during the nights when, after all those years of marriage, she missed having him nearby. Sundays seemed the worst of times; that was when they had always felt closest while praying as a couple during church services. It had become too painful to attend the same fellowship without him, so Gerry looked elsewhere. Discovering that her former pastor had returned to town, she soon settled into his church family again.

One evening in New York State, my phone rang; it was Gerry. We had not spoken for months, so we caught up. During the chat, she asked, "Do you remember telling me about those flower-strewn mountains and how you somehow knew that they were on the outskirts of Heaven?" Well, I still believed that true and shared the same. "One night," Gerry continued, "I asked the Lord if all was well with Stephen. Then, identically to the way He had in the hospital, Jesus took me to the grassy meadow flooded with flowers at the base of that majestic mountain.

"Looking up the slope toward its distant crest, I saw a human figure erect and facing away from me. At once, I was standing alongside Stephen and following his gaze into the valley below. There in all its glory was the shining city, not reflecting light from the sun but radiating a brilliance of its own from within. Shafts of light climbed vertically to hundreds of feet above its buildings, where they were abruptly cut off as if by a Heavenly barber's shears. Even from a distance, I could clearly see the intricacies of the Middle Eastern architecture. I knew about the streets of gold but never realized until that moment that the city was pure gold itself. Later, I did a Bible search of the Book of Revelation, where the Word says, "And the city was pure gold, like transparent glass" (Rev. 21:18).

"During our time together," Gerry went on, "Stephen never spoke, nor did we acknowledge each other's presence. It was clear to see that the city had his entire attention and was drawing him intensely. Then, without warning, he began to descend the mountain. My dear husband loved Jesus as much as anyone I have ever known."

She finished, "I had earlier confidence in my mind that he was in Heaven; now it was a fact settled in my heart. Receiving this assurance, I found myself resting in bed."

"You were right, you know," Gerry added emphatically as a final aside, "Heaven was on the far side of those mountains."

Wow, didn't that story end with a Kiss from Heaven for both of us?

Postscript

This little trilogy on Heaven is such a lovely demonstration of how the Lord will gift us all in the body for the common good (1 Cor. 12:7). My original Kiss from Heaven, staged in the outskirts of Heaven (which took place in the mid-1970s), to my knowledge never touched the lives of others following Darlene's memorial service until thirty years later in 2005. As promised, God's Word did not return to Him void (Isa. 55:11) but fulfilled His purpose when Gerry not only entered my original vision ill with Guillain-Barré syndrome but again four years later when seeking confirmation of her deceased husband Stephen's well-being.

The latter instance completed the circle and confirmed what I suspected over three decades earlier: Heaven lay secure beyond the locked arms of those verdant wildflower-laced mountains. Questioning if this last vignette might be a little theologically risky regarding the whole separation of the living from the dead issue, I concluded if Jesus and His disciples met with Elijah and Moses on the Mount of Transfiguration and Lazarus gave a holler to Abraham across that divide, why couldn't Gerry join Stephen for a moment to bring peace surrounding her husband's well-being in Heaven? I'm not sure where Stephen had been hanging out since he passed, but it appears as if the Lord either put a hold on his trip to the city until Gerry could view it with Him, or it was a timely Heavenly rerun (toward my leaning), alongside which the Lord would position her to bring the peace and confidence she needed.

Let us leave that to the theologians. What we can depend upon is Jesus having compassion for the downcast and the distressed among us when we end up like sheep without shepherds (Matt. 9:36)—and then doing something marvelous about it.

QUESTION: Where is the Kiss from Heaven in this God Story?

ANSWER: Stephen loved Jesus more than most. It showed. Sometimes he shined. The rest of the time, he glowed. For him, death was little more than an easy transition; for Gerry, there was nothing easy about it. So, Jesus, who has a special place in His heart for widows, did something wonderous and benevolent—another supernatural journey for Gerry by outer vision beginning in that familiar flower-strewn valley on the outskirts of Heaven to ascend a mountain where she would watch Stephen complete his journey to Jesus. So didn't Gerry receive yet another Kiss from Heaven—the peace she needed and, bless her heart, confirmation of what I had for years suspected: Our eternal city was just over that hilltop?

On A Wing and A Prayer (1965)

As a bustling little military town deep in South Texas, stuck indiscriminately between San Antonio and Corpus Christi, Beeville aptly lived up to its name. Its skies swarming with still-serviceable Korean War vintage F-9 Cougars and F-11 Tigers and fighters affectionately dubbed the "Grumman iron works" (based on those aircrafts' frequent willingness to extend airmen chances to walk away from emergency landings on terrain other than runways), Beeville was one of two overcrowded Naval Air Advanced Training Command facilities in the State of Texas teeming with dedicated young Navy and Marine officers. Upon completing eighteen months of ground school and flight curriculum, these warriors would earn their "wings of gold," the coveted emblem worn over the hearts of designated United States Naval aviators. It was 1965; the Vietnam conflict was accelerating, and new pilots were in heavy demand.

For our growing family, it had been an intense journey punctuated by four moves, beginning with the United States Marine Corps Officer Candidate School (OCS) in Quantico, Virginia. Negotiating the rigors of primary training in Pensacola, Florida, followed by basic jet in Meridian, Mississippi, we then moved back to Pensacola and the USS Lexington for training in carrier operations. Then, having added one daughter and soon another, we were about to finish and leave Beeville for the fleet.

In the military service, the old-timers rightfully prophesy, "Three moves equal one fire." About to move for the fifth time in less than two years, we were ready to settle down at a Marine facility, if only to confirm that "prophecy" by furnishing a new home. In a single heartbeat, I had snatched the opportunity to become a Naval aviator when the escalating Vietnam conflict required the Department of the Navy to augment its pilot population. Momentarily, I would be a proud and grateful addition to those ranks, making all the inconveniences during the last eighteen months well worth our family's effort.

A War Brat

As a child growing up during World War II, with a bobbysoxer sister ten and crewcut brother eight years my senior, I had known, if only by rubbing shoulders through my siblings, teen heroes volunteering for military duty in the years following Pearl Harbor. Soon, the entire country experienced a real and stifling war economy, with the government rationing everything from meat to tires, gasoline, nylons, shoes, and much more. The war machine needed copper so badly that pennies became zinc, steel, or reduced in copper content with a red hue; believe this or not, the feds even experimented with red plastic. None of the above were worth a "red cent." Entrepreneurial small-time black-market dealers were available when one could not get essential items. Any activity in that arena was supposed to be out of sight and hush-hush. So, as a little kid, if I saw something, I knew nothing.

The elder brother of my father was an Army Air Force bird colonel stationed in Nome, Alaska, where, the family understood, he commanded the US Coast and Geodetic Survey's mapping of the Pacific theater during the war. One day, he and his aircrew made an abbreviated visit to our local airbase, Hancock Field, in Syracuse, New York, with his personal B-25 Mitchell bomber. Dark olive Army green and sporting those identifying giant white stars and bar insignias on her wings and fuselage, that beauty arrived one crisp autumn day on the tarmac alongside my family, fingers firmly plugged into every ear, with engines howling like mad dogs spoiling for a fight. Up close and personal and coming to a halt, she bristled—a porcupine with stem-to-stern machine gun turrets manned by bigger-than-life flight crew dressed in high-altitude cold-weather leather flight gear lined with lamb's wool. In one split second, that nasty Mitchell seduced me to become a part of her world. By the end of that day, it was a done deal.

By the end of the month, I had assembled from scrap lumber in my dad's workshop a scaled-down, somewhat unrecognizable (hey, I was only five) mockup of that bird, nailed it to the swing seat hanging by three-quarter-inch hemp ropes from a giant maple in the side yard, and was flying three hops a day. Taking on bogies in enemy territory, within forty-eight hours, I became the youngest aviator to become an ace (an aviator with five kills) in United States Army Air Force history.

Sharing a bedroom with only my brother—our wallpaper riddled with Japanese Zeros mixing it up with a hive of F-4F Wildcat US Navy fighters—was the figurative beginning of military service for the both of us. A six-by-six-foot world map pasted on the wall between our twin beds let him pinpoint all America's battles reported nightly over our family's big RCA console radio nestled at the far end of the living room downstairs. It was there, sprawled evenings on a lush oriental rug, that we would anxiously await newscaster Gabriel Heater's vividly portrayed word pictures of that day's military action, worlds away but well within the reaches of that giant map stuck to our second-floor bedroom wall.

Life, Time, Colliers, and *Saturday Evening Post* magazines, stacked neatly on Mom's coffee table, portrayed graphically woven, colorful photographs of the war's bloody struggles among more mundane human interest stories or tempting advertisements the likes of Old Gold or Chesterfield cigarettes, Royal Crown Cola, or Blackjack gum as attempts to integrate the war's carnage into a semblance of daily normalcy. Even to a four-year-old kid, this oil-and-water approach seemed a little surreal without even knowing what that word meant.

Sadly, a few of the town's families, after pulling their window shades, would display small banners, gold star service flags, shocking our world with the reality of war by posting the loss of a loved one. Tiny olive drab replicas of tanks, jeeps, personnel carriers, ships, and planes filled Christmas stockings, while stuffed rabbits at Easter touted military garb. Popular songs like Glenn Miller's "American Patrol," "Boogie Woogie Bugle Boy" by the Andrews sisters, and others like "Praise the Lord and Pass the Ammunition," "Don't Sit Under the Apple Tree," and "I'll Be Home for Christmas" kept the war effort on the forefront of our ruminating minds. Listening to newsboys on the nearby streets of Syracuse hawking dailies displaying banner headlines of battles won or lost—while touting newspaper articles meant to unite all America against her common foes by labeling our enemies as Japs, Krauts, and Wops, all subhuman species capable of unspeakable atrocities—kept the entire city focused on the war. This was life for a kid growing up in the 1940s war years.

It was in that turbulent atmosphere of GI Joe, Tokyo Rose, Rosie the Riveter, Hitler, Tojo, Mussolini, Stalin, Churchill, FDR, MacArthur, and Eisenhower where patriotism and nationalism became the driving forces to keep citizens closely connected with a strenuous and sacrificial struggle. Those forces shaped deeply held opinions espousing the unerring righteousness of the United States of America and kept hearts knitted to her military forces willing to impose that righteousness on any country that would threaten or reject freedom for its people. Fascism, socialism, and communism soon became anathemas to this red-white-and-blue-blooded American boy, all too soon to become a young man.

Was it surprising each year's parade celebrating Memorial Day following the war found me riding a fender-less hand-me-down bicycle liberally emblazoned with "Old Glories" lashed to its scarred frame by electrical tape? With handlebars and spokes weaved through and through with rolls of red, white, and blue crepe paper, the bike and I would perform figure eights in formation with a handful of friends to the rousing cadence of a marching band leading a host of honored veterans. Marginally stuffed into their not-so-old military uniforms, our heroes paraded down deliriously cheering streets only to suddenly but solemnly discharge ten-gun salutes honoring their childhood companions turned fallen comrades buried in one of our town's two cemeteries.

Nor was it a surprise that my brother entered the Naval service after graduating from college. Ten years later, after completing college and working for a pharmaceutical company, I simply could not resist the "harpies' call," this time coming from Vietnam. Here, as I saw it, was another righteous conflict entered by an America willing to assume a mantle to defend freedom and defeat the scourge of communism from dominating the free world. Could I resist this honorable call to arms, in my mind the most noble of all? Impossible. Look, I was a child of World War II, an aspiring warrior from the very days of my youth. Would I deny myself a place to serve among my heroes or to fight beside my brothers? Never.

The Check Ride

There was my name and flight sandwiched between dozens of others on the ready room's scheduling board. It was a paradox, an auspicious yet foreboding occasion; my heralded final flight of the training command, which would earn me those coveted wings of gold, was assigned to an older Navy lieutenant commander—not only dissatisfied with his assignment to the training command, as were most instructors missing combat, but genuinely hostile to Marine students.

Though I'd never flown with this officer, I did know of his reputation. That provoked in me determination. One more flight and I would have those wings of gold. Nothing would thwart this Marine's effort. Besides, it was a gunnery check; what was there to do but perch 2000 feet above and abeam the tow plane, roll in on the banner streaming yards behind, and finally impregnate the latter with fifty caliber rounds? The gunnery average I carried was not that outstanding, but I could hold my own. *So, suck it up*, I thought, *deal with it. Tonight, Marine, we celebrate.*

A "section" is a flight of two aircraft, a leader and his wingman. With two Grumman F-11 Tigers, the instructor and I, one after another lighting afterburners, launched and turned south toward a restricted area set aside for gunnery practice over the Gulf of Mexico. It was a beautiful, clear June morning with little haze but a sky shotgunned with innumerable pint-sized clouds unlike any day I had seen.

Finding the tow plane 2000 feet below and to the left of my perch was a problem from the beginning. The sky, chock full of those cotton balls, offered me little to no chance to pinpoint my quarry. Repeatedly losing sight of the leader required us to rendezvous at certain predetermined points and altitudes, only to lose sight as I again reached the perch. The instructor cut the flight short and ordered me back to base on my own to await his return.

The lieutenant commander Navy instructor was not a happy camper; rather, he was in a rage. It had been an unsatisfactory flight; he made certain of that. He also made an inarguable point: I could not complete the mission. On that day, I question whether the Red Baron or Pappy Boyington could have conquered that cluttered sky to fly a satisfactory check ride. There was little to say but grudgingly accept the "down" (a failing grade for the hop and only the second of my entire time in training) and be scheduled for a refly. Tomorrow's weather would be clear, I assured myself, and the flight a piece of cake.

"Lieutenant," he growled, "I am not giving you a down." Isn't it wonderful how fast you relax when things suddenly turn around for good? Instantly, I changed my mind; that instructor was a good guy despite his past behavior. Unfortunately, my freedom from anxiety was short-lived as his voice cut short my whimsical self-talk: "I am asking for a speedy board."

He could not be serious. This was impossible; I could not fathom what I was hearing. That meant this Marine-hating *squid* (the Marine Corps pet name for a sailor) was intending to wash me out, accuse me unfit to fly, and steal my future as a Naval aviator. Closing in on two years of grueling blood, sweat, and tears and on the verge of life's greatest triumph, this bitter Marine hater was determined to deny my dream. What could I do? Nothing. Be a man, a Marine, and accept your fate. Intuitively, I knew better than to reason with this angry officer; if as vengeful as reputed, it would simply escalate his resolve and turn his intentions to concrete.

The lieutenant commander scheduled my Board of Inquiry for Fitness for the next morning. To this above-average student pilot, failure had never been part of the equation. Heading home, I was confused, humiliated, and dreading to tell my wife.

The Speedy Board

The speedy board met at precisely 0800 hours. In a summer tan uniform, I sat stiffly at the end of sixteen feet of polished table, each side lined by a half-dozen formally dressed officer instructors. The squadron's executive officer, Commander Pritchard, waited sternly and stiffly at the table's far end. Feeling like a sheep headed for slaughter, I wondered, *Was this to be my Alamo?* With no arguable defense (the hop had been what the hop was), the whole scenario felt more like walking the plank and the board a mere rubber stamp to deep-six a dangerous student pilot with a severely subpar performance. This lieutenant had no cards to play. Commander Pritchard had a royal flush.

With my self-esteem shaken and confidence levels near rock bottom, Executive Officer Pritchard prepared to address the board.

A Little More History

Fayetteville, a small village found in Central New York seven miles east of the Syracuse city limits, would grow in population from its few hundred citizens in the early 1940s to a sprawling suburbia of thousands by the late 1950s. Before World War II, my parents bought, for back taxes, the area's original homestead erected well before the Revolutionary War. Years later, the dwelling would become a veteran of the Underground Railroad and, even later, home to President Grover Cleveland's sister Rose. In 1940, while yet a vacant, rundown, and rambling structure sporting white clapboards with dark green shutters, it became our family's permanent residence.

Located one block north of the town's only intersection to boast an overhanging and eternally blinking red traffic signal, my bedroom wall became the nightly target of its blinkity-blink light for nearly two decades. In the early years, so infrequently used was that intersection that our family's elderly springer spaniel would commonly nap directly beneath the signal—as it was the only spot where a spring sun could penetrate the overlying canopy of interlocking old-growth maple and elm branches to warm the asphalt below. It's hard to believe the east–west highway, Route 5, participating in that intersection, was the busiest road across the entire midsection of New York State. Times have changed, have they not?

The original contractors built our historic house over a cellar carved six feet deep into solid limestone while framing it from massive timbers hand-hewn by drawshaves held in place by hardwood pegs alone. Overhead lay floors of sixteen-inch clear pine boards secured side by side with cherry wood butterfly joints. No metal nails were part of the entire original construction. Sitting on a large corner lot strewn with elaborate flower gardens, the home boasted colonial pillars with picketed porches running around half its perimeter. It also introduced all corners to Elm Street, a one-half-mile-long stretch of village tree-lined asphalt running west and leading down a precipi-tous slope to the "bottom of the hill" part of our town.

The Speedy, Speedy Board

"Lieutenant," Commander Pritchard began, his tone modulated by that unmistakably professional, deep "command voice" exercised by military officers about to assert their authority, "Is it true that you are from the Northeast?"

The answer I gave was in the affirmative.

"Do I see that you are from a town in Upstate New York by the name of Fayetteville?" he continued.

I, again, answered that was accurate.

Why is he doing this? I thought, *What has this to do with anything*?

"Did your family live on the corner of Elm and Manlius Streets?"

Now confused, I responded to this question with a firm, "Yes, sir."

"This board is dismissed," announced the commander with finality.

"Lieutenant, please be here at 0800 hours tomorrow morning prepared to refly yesterday's hop." He rose, followed by the rest—the now-puzzled officers as a sign of protocol and respect—and left the room. Baffled but more so relieved beyond words, I followed the equally confused flight instructors from the room. The lieutenant commander requestor of the board was beet-red furious again, re-fusing to look me in the eye on our way out. The instructor assigned me throughout my tour at Beeville, a Marine first lieutenant whom I highly respected, gave me a congratulatory slap on the back. Talk about a mindbender!

On a Wing and a Prayer

Commander Pritchard cleared up this mystery the following morning before our preflight brief. He, believe this or not, had spent his youth in Fayetteville, New York, living on that elaborately tree-shaded Elm Street but nearer the "bottom of the hill" part of town. Although two or three years her senior, Commander Pritchard had known my sister and occasionally walked her to school before graduating and enlisting in the Navy toward the end of World War II. Who could fathom that? Not me. What were the chances of a hometown family friend ending up as the executive officer presiding over my speedy board? Even more astonishing, that meeting happening half a country away, two decades removed, and two wars later! As wanting for answers as they were, those questions would have to wait; the commander had begun his preflight brief, and we had a hop to fly.

An hour later, after shaking my hand and graciously appreciating my skills, he gave an above-average grade for a flawless (or so he said) refly. Then, during the following morning's ceremony, above the left breast pocket of my Marine summer tan uniform, he pinned a bright and shiny set of gold aviators' wings. With no small thanks to Commander Pritchard, a whole lot of help from my instructors, friends, and family—and, in retrospect, a whole lot of glory to our God for an uncloudy sky—I earned those long-coveted wings of gold. Proudly, I was now a United States Naval aviator assigned to the United States Marine Corps.

Postscript

Like a bride ditched by her one and only, it was happening again. Eighteen months earlier, just two weeks before graduating from the Marine officer's candidate school at Quantico and a planned departure for the Naval air station at Pensacola to begin flight training, the Marine Corps informed me that an eye condition, a hyperphoria, would keep me from entering the aviation pipeline.

Crestfallen, I sought to adapt to this life-changing reality in part by watching weekly episodes of "The Lieutenant," a popular television show depicting a Marine second "looey" ground pounder in Vietnam, which our drill instructors encouraged on Friday nights. After each episode, it was clear that shifting gears into this new arena of jungle warfare would take more than a television series on Friday evenings. *So suck it up, Marine!* Then, another sudden change, and I was off to the Bethesda Naval Hospital and given a waiver by the ophthalmologist to reenter the aviation pipeline. As abruptly as I was out, I was back in. That's right—the wedding was back on.

Now, here we go again. After eighteen months of intense flight training, I faced an even more significant rejection, one with substantially more impact. It was the day before our nuptials. After living together for nearly two long years, my relationship with aviation was already a figurative marriage. Tomorrow, we would tie the official knot. The monogrammed United States Marine Corps dinnerware, camouflage towels, Department of the Treasury checks into the joint account, and his and her Naval aviator license plates were momentarily on order. This breakup could not be happening for a second time. After pushing through four moves, countless stressful hours in the cockpits of four unique aircraft, the decks of two aircraft carriers, and with only twenty-four hours separating our family from the most auspicious of days, the military planned to reject me again—and this time at the altar.

Flying an unsatisfactory check ride, the wedding would be off. Someone needed to show up, save me from myself, and guide us through that flight. That is no different in everyday life, is it? Eventually, we all need a helping hand to keep us flying straight and level. How often would I later face failing a check ride in my life's journey? When the marriage struggled, when a child went sideways, when the job did not pan out, or when my relationship with Heaven was on the skids, I would so often pull out the ever-present toolbox and try to fix each breakdown in my own strength. That was rarely enough. Don't you agree that following enough failures and tough times or even under more routine circumstances, we find ourselves tempted to take the "down" and quit rather than refly the hop and finish the course? Whatever the requirements to keep our love affair with life flying high, without a mercy person to save us from ourselves (or others) and guide us through a successful refly, we will end up grounded.

How often has Jesus our Savior stepped in unnoticed to assume the controls of our lives when we were in figurative bingo fuel states, metaphorical tentacles of monster thunderstorms, or allegorically stuck in an out-of-control burning aircraft with no foreseeable way out? In retrospect, a whole lot more times than we will admit, don't you think? If not, keep reading this book to its end.

Then, are we always aware of how He extricates us from those out-of-control circumstances? Now, I cannot speak for you, but rarely has this man been anything but clueless. On this occasion, however, there was neither smoke nor mirrors; this rescue was straightforward, clear as a bell, and plain as apple pie when Jesus, disguised as an old family friend in full Navy commander's regalia, pinned on my shiny wings of gold and, with them, bestowed another Kiss from Heaven.

Have you a better explanation? Bet yours is not so mercifully God. Should be, since "He saved us, not on the basis of deeds which we have done in righteousness, but according to His mercy" (Titus 3:5). Amen.

QUESTION: Where is the Kiss from Heaven from this God Story?

ANSWER: How about my sister's high school friend, with whose family we shared homes on the same street, one-half a country away in 1945, and who in 1965 became the senior officer on my Navy Board of Inquiry for Fitness—only to cancel the inquiry, schedule a refly of my final flight of the Naval Air Training Command, award an above-average grade, and the following morning pin on my Naval aviator's wings? More so, who could have known this God Story would jumpstart an unheard-of time of military service—with nearly 1500 hours of flight time in an A-4 Skyhawk jet tactical aircraft, ten months of Mediterranean cruise aboard the Carrier USS Independence (CVA 62) with the Marine Squadron VMA 324 (Vagabonds), a tour in Chu Lai, Vietnam, with the Marine Squadron VMA 223 (Bulldogs)—and culminate with three years as the flight surgeon for the United States Navy Fighter Weapons School (Top Gun) in NAS Miramar, California.

The Real Thing (1965)

The United States Marine Corps mandates training to prepare its officers and troopers to evade or escape capture while negotiating their way through enemy territory to safety. One Thursday, after two hours of instruction, the officer in charge paired us into two-man teams, each consisting of an officer with one enlisted Marine. Each team was issued a map, canteen, matches, compass, survival knife, and a parachute to serve as a makeshift shelter. Food was, in the Marine vernacular, a "personal problem." The only edict issued by the brass was that we take none with us. A team had two days to find its way from a desolate point of departure to its arrival over very uninhabitable terrain.

From my first tour as a Marine aviator assigned to a fixed-wing attack squadron, VMA 324, flying A-4E Skyhawks out of MCAS (Marine Corps Air Station) Beaufort, South Carolina, comes this little tale. The year was 1965, and although the Vietnam conflict was in full swing, my tour of duty in Southeast Asia would wait for our squadron's completion of a ten-month deployment to the Mediterranean Sea aboard the attack Carrier USS Independence, CVA-62. In retrospect, our escape & evasion (E&E) training turned out to be more challenging than storming the Mediterranean beaches of Barcelona, Cannes, Palma de Majorca, and others—which, to my knowledge, no Marine in history has ever tried to escape or evade. However, I have met a squad or two that, given the opportunity, may have avoided the shores of Chu Lai, Da Nang, Phou Bai, and others bordering the South China Sea. And let us not forget vets left over from WWII's Normandy, Iwo Jima among many others, and Korea's Inchon landings.

A Cold Day in Hades

Paired with a young squared-away lance corporal, we began our trek through the sprawling South Carolina marshlands a couple of miles inland from the Atlantic coast and hours removed from our airbase. Dreary and chillier than usual, the winter weather lost a little of its severity that day after we wisely quickened our pace in a move to break a sweat to stay warm. Dead reckoning was a breeze due to a plethora of reference points, which enabled us to cover more ground than expected during our first day's journey. Weaving among the scrubs, tramping through knee-high swamp grass, and negotiating ever-present small leads (meandering channels of sea water coming from the ocean) that intersected our path had us worn thin by the time we pitched camp for the night.

Fashioning poles from small trees with our lone survival knife to frame a parachute shelter as an admittedly poor imitation of a Native American teepee, we then gathered a small supply of wood, built a toasty fire in our tent's center, and hit the sack. The temperature plunged like a rock by midnight when we both woke shivering, chilled to the bone, and destined to spend the night gathering wood and stoking the fire. Packing up the chute at dawn, we set off on an intentionally brisk pace to thaw our bodies.

By ten o'clock, an anemic sun, contributing little heat to our frigid cause, was trying unsuccessfully to pierce the morning's ground fog clinging stubbornly to our path and refusing to bum off as we had expected. From the outset, it became increasingly difficult to find reference points to dead reckon our course. Unsuitably dressed for that day's wintry weather and with miles of walking ahead, our energy demand quickly exceeded our supply. Developing voracious appetites without food caused both of us to become increasingly fatigued, progressively lethargic, and a tad irritable (Well, I will take the rap for that one.). The recent depletion of our energy stores, a route complicated by fog, colder than usual weather, and an increased number of leads to circumnavigate successfully combined to turn yesterday's sprint into today's snail's pace.

Buried Treasure

We had exhausted the previous day's surplus miles and were falling behind the projection for the day, having but three or four more hours to cover the remaining terrain. Our conversations had deteriorated to oxygen-preserving essentials like "wait up" or "slow down," while our appetites, punctuated by frank refusals from our bodies to "suck it up" and "get over it," had become our primary adversaries. Wishfully, in silence, I pleaded, "If we only had some sugar, life would take on new meaning."

How far were we from civilization? Who knew? Our map lacked any sign of a settlement, town, or city from the beginning. So here we were, yet in the "boonies," at least two miles from the ocean, walking these eternally boring grassy flats notched by those obstructive leads and hoping beyond hope to reestablish our preplanned route. The serpentine little channel of seawater, along which we were stumbling, yet another one trying to further impede our progress, appeared about ten feet wide and three feet deep; although I had spotted no aquatic life in its clear water, the bottom of this channel was unobstructed.

Wait one second! Eureka! Were my eyes deceiving me? Was this a mirage? Was it a visual hallucination? Dropping to my hands and knees, I peered over that lead's bank and into its crystal waters, confirming as genuine that which I had moments before held in wonder. It was nothing less than a miracle. Motioning for the lance corporal to join me, we both stared incredulously at today's Kiss from Heaven submerged below our feet. There, in the depths of our little lead, standing at rigid attention and braced against its steep bank like a private at office hours, was a full, unblemished, unmolested, and unopened sixteen-ounce glass bottle of classic Coca-Cola. That is right, Marine, an honest-to-goodness king-sized Coke, cooled to perfection, ready for consumption, and but one generous arm's length away!

"Lance corporal," I boomed in my best command voice, "it is indisputably time to marshal our forces!"

For the life of me, I cannot remember who held whose legs so that, partially submerged, the other could rescue that coveted soft drink. I can tell you this, however: We conducted that mission with precise Marine Corps teamwork, esprit de corps, and without a hitch. Then, in celebration, we split our booty equally, toasted a "semper fi" in unison, and with eight ounces of Coke injecting lifesaving jolts of killer white sugar and nerve-rattling caffeine into each of our thirsty bloodstreams, instantly picked up the pace to arrive at our intended destination with ample time and energy to spare.

Postscript

How did that virgin bottle of Coca-Cola find its way to that remotest of remote places? Did it wash in miles from the sea? Did it fall uninjured from a plane? Did a meandering lost soul carry it a day's walk from the nearest public road only to carelessly drop it into the lead? Each explanation sounds as ludicrous as the remaining two, doesn't it? But then, seeing was believing. There it had inexplicably been in its altogether improbable setting, a king-sized bottle of Coca-Cola spied by two "out of gas" Marines spent from an unexpectedly challenging escape and evasion training exercise.

Later, there was minimal chance I shared that story with my squadron mates. It was not worth the risk of them labeling me a prevaricator—or worse, a "wimp" to have needed other than a standard issue of Marine "can do" attitude to get our team through that E&E exercise (as if a Coke were steroids or a denigrated energy supplement we had imbibed). Of greater import, I may have, if not broken, at least faced an accusation of bending the code. We were not to take any semblance of food on our mission.

To have caught a fish or trapped an animal would have been justifiable, if not admirable, in the sight of the command. I'm not sure that "catching or trapping" a king-sized Coca-Cola shared the same legitimacy. But Jesus, our Savior, often on the sly, commonly acts like one, doesn't He? Laced throughout the scriptures, we find provision as one of God's specialties. Why even one of His names, Jehovah Jireh, translates to God, our provider. Fresh manna and quail from His hand sustained the Israelites for forty years in the wilderness on the way from Egypt to the Promised Land, water came from the rock at Moses' command, Jesus multiplied the loaves and fishes on the sea of Galilee and gave Peter a large catch before breakfast when no fish had been caught during an entire night's vigil. Elijah, hiding at the brook of Cherith, ate meat and bread brought by ravens twice a day, even as he had functioned as God's go-between provider to a widow and her family to miraculously see them supplied with an inexhaustible reserve of flour and oil. Why, then, should we have been surprised when a king-sized Coke showed up along our escape and evasion route?

Now, we are not putting ourselves in the class of Moses, Elijah, or Peter, but timely provision has been available over the years to believers in need. That provision is by no means limited to food and drink but also commonly covers other necessities of life. Years ago, while speaking with evangelist friends Tom and Deborah Glibe of FireGate Ministries, who live by faith, we discovered that they had sold their home and furnishings on the West Coast to obey a word from the Lord to move to Hawaii. Near penniless upon their arrival in the islands, they were right off the bat instructed by Holy Spirit to donate all but one offering during their following three weeks of meetings.

Stuck in the bowels of a hotel with their entire family, one morning Holy Spirit directed Mom to visit a jewelry shop in the hotel's lobby, where she prayed with a Christian woman hard at work as a clerk. Heaven fell as the hotel manager happened upon the scene; minutes later, with a little help from our evangelist and a whole bunch from Holy Spirit, the manager found herself in the arms of Jesus.

Well, it was not long before our friends were occupying two ocean-front rooms, shortly thereafter upgraded to the only penthouse suite in the entire hotel. Did I mention that, as I understood it, they stayed the entire time on the Lord's credit card? Are such stories rare? Not if you hang with those who live by faith. God's provision is easy to see when dramatic but sorely missed when we fail to attribute even routine provision for the basics in our lives to His grace. Think about it.

Doesn't He bestow Kisses from Heaven regularly in ways we do not notice—or, even if we do, take for granted? Wouldn't it bless our hearts if our eyes could see the unfathomable goodness of God for His provision in every minute area of our lives? If we learned to appreciate Him in this way, giving thanks for everyday provision of food and drink (Luke 11:3) before dining would take on even deeper significance.

Out of curiosity, dear Christian, when was the last time you bowed your head over a king-sized Coke?

QUESTION: Where is the Kiss from Heaven from this God Story?

ANSWER: Discovering that sixteen-ounce king-sized Coca-Cola in the boonies was unique and beyond any satisfactory explanation outside divine intervention in the dehydrated affairs of a couple of weather-beaten Marines. Why? Well, explain it as you will, a full sixteen-ounce bottle of Coke sinks like a rock when dropped in water.

But washed up two miles from the ocean by the tides in Carolina? That's hard to swallow (well, until opened, anyway). A glass object falling from an aircraft at terminal velocity onto water travels at 118 mph. Remember the last time you fell from your slalom ski going fifty? Whoa. What do you think—would it splash or splatter? And wouldn't any hiker intentionally crossing this forsaken place carry a lighter canteen? We could get into hypotheticals here, but hey, let's make it easy and assign this little Kiss from Heaven to the merciful One who arranged it.

A No Fly or Die Hop (1967)

For Marine aviators stationed at Chu Lai, Republic of Vietnam, in 1967, flights employing AN/TPQ-10 course direction radar were high-altitude bombing missions flown south of the DMZ (Demilitarized Zone) proximate to the city of Dong Ha on the South China Sea during nights or inclement weather. Do I have you located? Under control of a radar facility from the ground 20,000 feet below, these missions limited enemy troops, munitions, and equipment flowing from North Vietnam. Positioning by radar over those presumed targets enabled pilots to accurately deliver ordnance. The flight schedule announced this aviator was due for a TPQ launch at 0200 hours the following morning.

Monsoon season was in full force. That night's fierce winds were lashing at our hooch and driving warm tropical rain horizontally through its wide-open side panels. Their direction had also forced closure of our 8000 feet of primary runway for a crosswind strip measuring but 3000. The shorter runway ended within a couple of those feet from an imposing 100 feet of patiently waiting sand dune. That made it necessary to use a motorized land catapult to guarantee aircraft sufficient airspeed to achieve an altitude to clear its clutches on takeoff.

On this night, with the catapult regrettably—but as usual—out of commission, two JATO (jet-assisted takeoff) bottles, rocket canisters attached to the fuselage aft of both wings, would launch my heavily loaded Skyhawk over that sandy hump instead. Approaching 1500 hours of flight time, I had experienced but one rocket-assisted takeoff, and that was more like a funny-car-ride-turned-warp-speed NASA launch. It had been a rush. Parenthetically, that flight was under CADVU (clear and visibility unlimited) conditions during a beautiful day from a dry "flatter than a flitter" 10,000 feet of concrete runway at MCAS Yuma, Arizona. The monsoon torrent battering this night's undertaking aviators would dub an EBAW (even the birds are walking) weather condition and the uneven, short, crosswind runway surface more like motocross whoops. Going directly to the NATOPS (Naval Air Training Operations Systems) manual to review Skyhawk JATO operating procedures was my last step before struggling through the wind-driven rain toward the flight line and to that night's out-of-the-ordinary hop.

Ride 'Em, Woody, Ride 'Em

Blown about the tarmac by those relentless monsoon winds, while pelted by firehose torrents of horizontal rain during a quick preflight inspection, an unrecognizable plane captain, shrouded by a wind-swept poncho twice his size, helped fire up the "Scooter" (an affectionate name given the versatile little aircraft by her pilots). Then, the bird and I, having received taxi instructions, inched toward that unfamiliar crosswind runway. Constantly buffeted by the uninterrupted onslaught, the intrepid little aircraft paused but briefly beside the dimly lit and near-invisible RDO (runway duty officer) shack before taking the runway. A Major Cooney—or, by chance, Looney (that should tell you something right off the bat about that night)—huddled within its dark interior and cleared us for an unclear takeoff.

Hidden in the blackness ahead lay 3000 feet of unlit, undulating, interlocked aluminum alloy plates, joined to one another and resting uncomfortably upon ever-shifting sands. Their Marine green nonskid painted surfaces had long ago worn thin, exposing extensive areas of perilously slick and shining bare metal reflecting the aircraft's taxi light. The purchase on this runway's matting was no issue when a catapult securely gripped an aircraft on launch or the plane was later recovered by a reliable arresting gear (like those used aboard a carrier). This dark morning, however, under these daunting weather conditions, the bird and I would have to negotiate that slippery surface on our own. Mentally reviewing the launch procedure, I hurried through the preflight checklist, armed the JATO system, jammed the throttle to the fire wall, and released the brakes.

The fully "loaded for bear" Skyhawk began her journey down the roller-coaster runway, her taxi light straining to pierce the curtain of torrential rain concealing the windswept strip shrouded in the inky darkness ahead. When the aircraft reached the designated knots of speed to assure rudder control, I punched the JATO button on the throttle's stabilizer handle to activate the rockets. Expectedly, the bird cooperated by surging forward like a 1970s muscle car; unexpectedly, the rapidly accelerating Skyhawk also entered a yaw to the left, quickly unresponsive to full right rudder, and then increasing right brake pressure.

The sound behind confirmed ignition, so why was the aircraft suddenly in a slow but relentless counterclockwise rotation toward the left margin of the flooded runway? While running a quick mental scan of my options, I helplessly watched the sand beyond the runway's edge drawing closer and closer, now rapidly approaching at a forty-five-degree angle. The speeding and out-of-control Skyhawk, brakes now uselessly locked with wheels hydroplaning across the slick, polished metal runway, was regrettably moving at speeds less than the 120 knots necessary to safely egress the aircraft by ejection while on the ground.

To make things worse, she carried 500-pound bombs, three full tanks of fuel, spewed fire from multiple orifices and, headstrong as she had become, was determined to carry us into a waiting coffin of sand. The Skyhawk had become an explosion looking for a place to happen, was acting as if she had found one, and left me but three seconds to solve a serious conundrum. With no time to jettison anything, I shut the engine down (in a presumptive but wishful effort to prevent an inevitable fire) and reached to retract the landing gear. Going into the sand with a hot engine was untenable, but then, what was not?

Throughout the short but rapid evolution of this crisis, I could hear the RDO constantly urging me on over the radio like a wild-eyed rodeo dad, "Ride 'em, Woody, ride 'em!"

A Second Chance

Resigned to my fate (it is hard to be altogether ready to become a fireball), without warning and in less than an actual heartbeat, the plane spun violently clockwise a full ninety degrees and quickly accelerated once again, now at forty-five degrees from the opposite side of the runway. Then I got the picture. To begin this conundrum, the port (left) JATO bottle had fired on its own, causing an asymmetric thrust and uncontrollable left yaw magnified by the glassy, smooth, wet runway. With no time left, the fresh starboard (right) rocket, kicking in as we were about to plunge into eternity, took advantage of that slick, wet surface to spin the hydroplaning aircraft like a nickel a fully ninety degrees in the opposite direction. The Scooter was approaching the centerline when I gained solid rudder control. Back on course and quickly pushing 100 knots, the aircraft was gaining speed straight down the runway; regrettably, it had no functioning engine and inadequate speed to eject, but a working JATO bottle determined to run us into that upcoming but to date invisible "hump."

Here was our new set of options: We were comfortably under directional control but still beneath safe ejection speed. We might jettison the blazing starboard rocket (of that I was not certain) to slow down, but at what cost? If the jettisoned rocket did not strike the aircraft's wing, fuel cell, or canopy, just ahead on the summit of that imposing dune were hooches housing countless sleeping Marines, Americal Division Army troops, and a few ROKs (Republic of Korea) Marines vulnerable to any rocket cutting an uncontrolled swath among them. Also, at the dune's base was an occupied line shack where aviators filled out and maintenance personnel processed "yellow sheets" before and after flights.

Deciding the option with the least risk was to let well enough alone and choose, instead, to let the present rocket burn out as the first had while depending upon the emergency overrun gear to trap the aircraft. So our journey continued relentlessly on its uncertain, stormy path. Despite the outcome, this hop was a no-fly, one way or another.

At the not-so-far end of the runway, at the base of that immovable mountain of sand, was an unseen emergency overrun gear. As primitive as the system appeared, less than two inches of steel cable elevated three or more inches above the matting by sections of used car tires, it had proved highly dependable. However, the Skyhawk had one significant issue: When an aviator lowered her arresting hook to meet the slick, uneven runway, added nitrogen gas snubber pressure was designed to prevent it from skipping the cable. Unfortunately, the runway surface, irregular as it was, carried a high potential to cause even a well-pressurized hook to bounce. That one bounce could escalate into a series, each increasing in amplitude, and almost guaranteed the hook to skip the cable. The plane would then stop, but only after we had finally confronted that formidable dune mano-a-mano.

By hesitating to lower the hook until the last moment, I hoped to eliminate or at least reduce the number of bounces, reduce the risk of a hook skip, and improve our chances of engaging the wire. With little help from the dimming taxi light, I barely caught sight of the approaching overrun gear dimly illuminated in a swiftly closing space. At that last moment, after snapping the hook handle down and forward, the aircraft—heavily laden with explosive ordinance, a full load of fuel, a JATO bottle spewing fire, and rocketing at more than 100 knots—snagged that cable, extended the overrun gear a nose hair from its limit, and stopped with the fuel probe inches from that sand dune.

Canopy popped, I unstrapped and slid down the wing, past the spent port rocket, and onto the overrun. Flickering light issued eerily from the starboard side of the bird where the still-grumbling but dying JATO canister was now spending itself by coughing flames. When it died, only torrential rain, whipping wind, and total darkness separated us from where this shenanigan had begun. Altogether fine with that outcome was this aviator. Altogether fine.

Any Hop You Walk Away From

For the first and only time in my career, I passed up the line shack, did not place the bird in a down status with "gripes" (mechanical failures), and intentionally "forgot" to sign off the yellow sheet, which would have to wait until the not-too-distant light of day. Visibly upset I was not, nor would I let my dissatisfaction show. But beneath the deep numbness rumbled a volcano poised to erupt, and the last thing needed for those maintenance shack troopers was to see my unprofessional inner self. That incident should never have happened. By daybreak, with composure regained, I was ready for a day at the office.

Aviators live in heavy denial to survive such events, which merely ready them for the next. My near miss with death went unnoticed. Do not be surprised; everyone in that business knows, but for the grace of God, there go I. Assuming a wiring error by an inexperienced Marine ordinance trooper caused this near miss (but who knew), I deposited the whole mess in the maintenance officer's lap, who assured me he would check the equipment and bring any offender up to speed. It was just one complex incident unaddressed by specific NATOPS emergency procedures but relying on good headwork by the aviator and a whole lot of good fortune from above. On such occasions with multiple contributing factors, everyone, except the safety officer from whom there was no sound, recognizes that any hop you walk away from is a good hop.

Postscript

Aviators might assign this incident or any like it to misfortune followed by good karma. Others could say untenable circumstances or inadequate equipment managed by skill and good headwork. Then count the naysayers to chime in with pilot error and dumb luck. Can you imagine Father God, in an oversized poncho with his big index finger pushing against that Skyhawk's vertical stabilizer (tail), spinning the desperate plane ninety degrees away from sure carnage, and then moving aft to sweeten the pressure on her hook? Why not? Or how about one of those massive guardian angels on the way to a well-deserved R&R, dropping in to lend a hand before moving on to heavenly Hawaii? It hardly mattered. This Marine was fat, dumb, and happy again with his exquisitely timed Kiss from Heaven, and all was right with his world.

QUESTION: Where is the Kiss from Heaven from this God Story?

ANSWER: Are you aware there are four cables lined up in series to "trap" an aircraft landing on an aircraft carrier? Should you miss the first one (ideally you seek the third), three more are available. If you miss all four, then the deck is angled to allow the pilot time to add power, take flight, go around, and try again. That night in Chu Lai, there was but one "Rube Goldberg" rigged arresting cable, and to miss it meant nothing but a sandy grave.

There was no "go around and try again" in those cards. Even getting to the last-chance cable that night took a mathematically impossible complex Kiss from Heaven—a microsecond of ninety-degree twirl on a greasy runway preceded by a timed-to-the-nanosecond escape from a coffin of sand choreographed by a precisely timed ignition of that second JATO rocket secured to the starboard side of the aircraft . . . and all three together spanning less than one full second. We talk about an eleventh-hour God. How about an eleventh-hour, fifty-ninth minute, and fifty-ninth-second Jesus. Any questions as to Who pulled off this Kiss from Heaven?

A Heart Shaped Earring (1978)

Western Oregon rarely experienced a Christmas without inclement weather. So, as soon as we had opened our presents and eaten the holiday gobbler, the kids and I were looking for something to do for the rest of this unusually beautiful, albeit fading, Christmas afternoon. Taking the blue sky and warm sun as engraved invitations, two of the children—my oldest daughter, Melanie, fourteen, and my youngest son, John, nine—joined me in scaling the mountain just east of our home on Dorena Reservoir, ten miles southeast from the small city of Cottage Grove.

Oregon's mountains are not only rugged and steep but also lush with giant ferns and towering Douglas firs, which thrive on reliably abundant rains.

We began our ascent by pushing through those chest-high ferns, still moist from an early morning mist and glittering in the afternoon sun. Navigating through a dense and dimly lit forest of massive firs commanding the incline ahead within the hour introduced a ridge reaching the summit. Then, plunging eagerly into a steep descent, our journey led us through ever-lengthening shadows into dying daylight and a darkening valley below. Without warning, a sprawling grove of magnificent oaks, hiding stealthily among their mighty fir counterparts, swallowed us. Shuffling through twelve or more inches of oak leaves littering the forest floor while dodging countless low-hanging branches of this dense hardwood refuge significantly slowed our passage. Bobbing, weaving, and then feeling our way through that web of limbs left us with a single goal: finding a way out of the forest before the darkness stole what light we had left.

Minutes later, my son and I entered a small clearing. By now, the surrounding mountains to the west were contesting the withering remnants of our afternoon sun, allowing few of its rays to pierce the surrounding trees. It was only then we realized my daughter was nowhere in sight. Anxiously, we pushed back through the thickening twilight, repeatedly calling her name. Only after a small lifetime did we find her secluded and silent among those oaks. I could barely see her tears through the dusk.

"What happened?" I heard myself ask.

Weeping, my daughter shared how she had entered the grove only to discover that one of her earrings was missing. Wishing to have her ears pierced as a Christmas present, her mother had not only agreed but also bought her a pair of lovely golden heart-shaped earrings; to her delight, she found those treasures under that morning's tree. Proudly, that special gift made her feel and act so much more mature. But now, with tears cascading down her face, the joy was gone, leaving only a devastated little girl behind. At such times, what can a father do with an aching heart like that? How about asking another inane question: "Where do you last recall having the earring?" I blurted, stumbling over what else to say.

Retracing her steps by memory was no help. Lost for words, she finally spoke. "I remember a branch brushing my head while walking through these trees."

Then, I requested she take us to that place.

Turning, she weaved her way, my son and I in tow, thirty feet back through the forest and then pointed. "I think it was somewhere in this area."

Catching up, my heart was sinking faster than the struggling sun.

Everything looked the same; in the fizzling light, all we had were dozens of trees with low-slung branches invading the space where we stood, boots immersed in an ocean of leaves.

Feeling powerless, as would any father unable to help his child at such a time, I asked if she could narrow down the branch's location. *Kind of an impossible question under the circumstances*, I silently thought, keenly aware that question was only a cowardly tactic to delay the inevitable.

"Maybe about here?" my daughter said, her voice in a crescendo as if she were asking a question.

As the day's light ended, so ended any hope left in my heart; I felt depressed. Well, the Word does say, "Hope deferred makes the heart sick" (Prov.13:12). That day, no truer words had been spoken. Yet I could not get myself to quit. I could not tell her the truth.

Positioned alongside the low-slung branch nearest her estimate, I began a trip to my knees into the dense carpet below. The abbreviated prayer sighed on my way down, as near as I can recall, went something like this: "Lord, you know my daughter loves you and you her. She is so brokenhearted over the loss of her precious earring. Lord, you know where it is hiding. Please, Jesus, would you find it for us?" With that, my knees hit the ground as if to punctuate my whispered prayer. Woefully, I admit, my faith tanked in unison beside them.

Why, I asked myself, *did I feel so compelled to stave off the inevitable?* Centering myself beneath the barely visible branch in question, I began to mechanically lift leaves aside one by one, slowly creating an ever-widening and deepening black hole. The afternoon's sunlight, now a memory, my work was in near darkness. Need I say that the bottomless black hole growing in that ocean of leaves was no competition for the emptiness filling my father's heart?

Bending low to draw closer to the recess, there was no way to see through the ten inches of ink to its base. Past ready and now resigned,

I murmured inaudibly but despondently, "What's the use, that earring could be anywhere along today's three-mile journey? Even if it has fallen among these bushy oaks, it is now irretrievably lost among countless millions of leaves."

It was time to quit.

At that precise moment (and I mean at that precise moment), at the pinnacle of my despair, a stray sliver of light, a nanosecond of laser dart from a dying sun somehow escaping a distant mountain, snuck over my left shoulder to pierce that black chasm. Another scant nanosecond's worth of glint sprung from its formless interior. Rudely awakened, my heart leapt alongside it. *Lord, could it be? Could it impossibly be?*

Carefully now, ever so carefully, I bent farther forward, face hovering as close as I dared to that ill-defined and unstable black hole. Nothing, I could see nothing. Gingerly, I probed the depths of that formless abyss. Nestled ten inches into the depths of its darkness, my fingers brushed a single oak leaf positioned horizontally across the hole's base. Holding my breath ever so cautiously, I slowly raised it close to my face. There, barely discernible but cradled in the arms of that little lone leaf, one among countless millions, lay a solitary little gold heart-shaped earring, my little girl's Christmas Kiss from Heaven.

Afterward, all we could do was holler and dance and thank Jesus, hug each other, and go bonkers over this unforgettable miracle of Jesus' love for a brokenhearted little girl and her desperate father. Years later, she gave me that earring; I cherish it to this day. It is impossible to look upon that little heart without seeing the big, merciful heart of a loving Father who was not too busy to pause and mend the wounded heart of His devastated little child with an impossible plight on a beautiful Christmas afternoon so many years ago. Christmas Kiss from Heaven received. Thank you so much, Lord.

Postscript

When my father lost something, which was rare, he would say: "It's like trying to find a needle in a haystack." Our adventure that day made it more like trying to find a needle in the entire state of Nebraska. What were the chances? Still, Jesus does not deal in chance; he deals in mercy—unfathomable mercy, the Bible might paint it. We can never plumb its depths. It is mercy without end, mercy that goes beyond the borders of forever. If there was ever a time when mercy reigned, where sorrow lasted for the night, but joy came in the morning—like that old woman wearied from sweeping her house to find that lost mite, the shepherd his lost lamb, and the father his prodigal son—this had to be it.

It is one thing to create everything, as the Bible tells us Jesus has done (John 1:3); it is yet another to keep track of it all. If I get through a day without losing the eyeglasses perched atop my only nose, it is a sign and a wonder. But in the gathering darkness of that fading Christmas Day when Jesus, hearing the mere whisper of a faith-starved prayer, reached into a galaxy of oak leaves to easily retrieve a few molecules of gold, I knew beyond reason that our Savior was God of the impossible (Mark 9:23) and that nothing, absolutely nothing, was needed but a mustard seed of faith (Matt.17:20) for any of us to see the goodness of God in the land of the living (Ps. 27:13).

QUESTION: Where is the Kiss from Heaven from this God Story?

ANSWER: To believe God is who He says He is needs only this single story. Forget the rest. No need. Listen—a golden heart-shaped earring lost somewhere along a three-mile journey, among maybe billions of leaves, with nightshades fallen, sought by a faithless father pleading for the Lord to dry his daughter's tears and then found by a Heavenly laser pointer? No way. Forget it. God has better things to do and better ways to do them. Well, wrong again, unbelieving one. When will we learn? "And looking upon *them* Jesus said to them, 'With men this is impossible, but with God all things are possible'" (Matt. 19:26). "Merry Christmas, baby girl." Love, Jesus.

A Shocker (1979)

The beginning of private medical practice was a tad stressful. In 1977, I agreed to join an emergency medicine group of six physicians contracting with a major hospital in Eugene, Oregon. Then, for no stated reason, the hospital's administration changed its mind, reversed course, and offered each physician salaried positions instead. It was not a matter of money but of trust that caused half of the physicians to seek employment elsewhere. What concerned those of us who had uprooted our families, traveled thousands of miles, and come in good faith was the reliability of this potential lifelong employer. Undaunted, we sought other means of work. Within two days, a position in family practice opened in Cottage Grove, a small city of 3,500, which sat twenty miles to the south but ten miles closer to the lovely home where our young family had settled on a butte overlooking the five glorious miles of Dorena Reservoir.

To make ends meet while building an accounts receivable in the new group family practice, I agreed to work every other Thursday through Sunday night from seven in the evening to seven the following morning at the same emergency room in Eugene I had recently spurned but which now had a similar need to our own. That mutual arrangement was one Jesus might have made, don't you think? That allowed me Mondays through Thursdays in the office, on call one weekend a month in my hometown, and the remaining one weekend a month with family. It would have to do for a while, though it lasted two full years until I entered solo practice.

Working that schedule was exhausting. Finding it impossible to catch up on sleep precipitated a real struggle. Among a myriad of other things arose the need to stay current with the ever-evolving medical literature. Ironically, the most impactful healthcare article that came across my path during those years was not from a medical journal but was discovered tucked away on the back page of Eugene's long-established newspaper, the *Register-Guard*. One morning, someone in our office threw a used edition onto the countertop in our nurses' station, where a brief back-page article caught my eye.

It dealt with a recent underreported phenomenon, toxic shock syndrome, increasingly found among menstruating women—most commonly using high-absorbency tampons—who developed sudden high fever, headache, and sore throat, which commonly progressed to a cluster of severe hypotension (low blood pressure), kidney failure, and clinical shock. The condition was so menacing as to require amputations in a growing number of women's extremities (due to the poor perfusion effects of shock) and, tragically, a mounting number of deaths.

The causal agent was unknown, but volume expansion with massive amounts of intravenous fluids, vasopressors (medications to raise blood pressure), and broad-spectrum antibiotics were the suggested treatments of choice.

How Things Change

Past midnight, I was busy working my twelve-hour shift in the emergency room. Fatigued after a long week in the office and hoping to steal a couple of hours of sleep before the night's end, that pipedream seemed unlikely with patients pouring in as they were. Congress had passed a bill years before, the Hill-Burton Act, lately applied to

emergency rooms, which mandated hospitals see all patients presenting at their doorsteps despite an inability to pay. Emergency medicine
was a fledgling specialty with full-time residencies and board-certified
physicians both rare. In the past, hospitals had rotated staff doctors to
share nights on call to cover their emergency rooms—and that, often
from home. On-call physicians who remained overnight in hospitals
often found an hour or two of sleep, a phenomenon rapidly facing
extinction.

Then, to the consternation of hospital financial officers, patients who could not pay or find time to see their family practi-
tioners during the day were now using ERs as nighttime convenience
clinics. Governmental intrusion into the medical system, while
well-intentioned and legal per the Hill-Burton Act, made it necessary for hospitals (I was so informed) to raise their rates elsewhere
(medical and surgical floors, operating suites, and intensive care
units) to cover increased expenses for the unpaid emergency services.
Understandably, insurance companies soon raised their rates on private medical insurance policies to cover those rising costs for both
inpatient and outpatient care. So hardworking private citizens like
John Smith (that would be you and me) ended up bearing the expenses
for the general public's care via our own increased health insurance
premiums.

That began a cycle of inflationary changes that have continued,
often resulting from the federal government mandating medical care
it was unwilling to fund and insurance companies independently deciding what they would pay. Believe me, the twenty-dollar doctor visit
to see a general practitioner in those days quickly became a distant
memory as had long before the three-dollar doctor's visit of my youth.
(The above is a brief historical nugget which, while applicable to times
past, may not apply currently but, regrettably, may.)

Kismet or Kiss

Out of the corner of my eye, I caught a pair of EMTs (emergency medical technicians) rolling a young female patient fresh from an ambulance into an examination room on a hospital gurney. Even from a distance, her blanched face and cyanotic skin (bluish because of oxygen deficit) were immediate cause for concern. According to the EMTs, a distraught mother had reported her daughter as being "perfectly normal" before complaining of a rapid onset sore throat, headache, and lightheadedness an hour before she called for help. The young woman had become progressively weaker and confused by the time she reached the hospital.

The EMTs' primary home examination found no readily accessible veins, the result of a precipitous drop in her blood pressure, which prevented the placement of an intravenous line outside the hospital to elevate her pressure. Now, absent a palpable pulse or blood pressure, unintelligible, and unresponsive to pain, she was facing an impending vascular collapse and severe shock by the time we had a deep subclavian line in place to begin volume expanders (IV fluids) and vasopressors (medications to raise blood pressure).

Contacting the internist on call to hospitalize the young woman was not a pleasant task but also no surprise. Who enjoys trekking to a hospital at 2:00 a.m.? Recalling that brief article on the back page of the local newspaper discarded on our office counter earlier that week, I shared with him there was a good possibility we had a case of toxic shock syndrome, unreported to date in the State of Oregon. Who knew?

His response was not a surprise or reassuring: "What the devil is toxic shock syndrome?"

Sharing what I knew in twenty-five words or less happily piqued the internist's interest (an easier task with new or rare diagnoses), which happily hastened his trip. His management of the young woman's tenuous course in the ICU was prompt and successful, as she eventually left the hospital with not only her life but all her limbs.

This may have been the first time in history that a diagnosis and treatment protocol for an unfamiliar life-threatening disease, this time toxic shock syndrome, would come from the back page of a discarded edition of a local newspaper. Fortunately, it was not too long before investigators isolated a toxin from a strain of staphylococcus bacteria as the causative agent for this dread condition, and an effective standard treatment protocol was published.

Postscript

Although we often use them, words like *coincidence, serendipity, kismet, karma, luck, chance, fate,* or *breaks* should not be part of a Christian's vocabulary. Our omnipresent Lord knows the beginning from the end. Who can hold anything from His sight or from His hand? Why were my eyes drawn to that newspaper article? Why was I on call that night when that young woman arrived at the emergency room? Were there other physicians who worked in our physician rotation who knew about this disease? Upon investigation, none. What might have happened had I not had the "clues" needed and missed the urgency of this condition unfamiliar to those parts of Oregon? Would that previously healthy young woman have faced amputation or death? Who could predict that?

Is it any wonder that the Lord brought a second case of toxic shock syndrome to our remote Cottage Grove office just days later? Vegas would not have put a nickel on those odds. But, as we now know, Jesus does not deal in odds; He deals in mercy. So, after my earlier ER watershed experience, it was hardly a surprise the Lord came to the rescue of a second critically ill woman in an office where, from the beginning, everyone would be singing from the same song sheet.

Make that a song sheet of praise, please. Withholding no gratitude from the *Register-Guard* for doing its reliably excellent work, shouldn't we first give credit where credit is due? Certainly. Thank you, Lord, for using your wonderful problem-solving ways incognito through the hands of a harried city editor, an early morning paperboy, an office nurse enjoying her morning pre-patient cup of coffee, and, in the nick of time, a sleep-deprived doctor attracted to the back page of a discarded daily newspaper proclaiming breaking medical news—soon to manifest serially as two young women's extraordinary life-preserving Kisses from Heaven.

QUESTION: Where is the Kiss from Heaven from this God Story?

ANSWER: I still get a few cold sweats or palpitations if I dwell on that night when a cyanotic young woman came to the ER forty-five years ago. There were so many links in that chain that could not fail for her to survive: 1) my immediate presence as the EMTs brought her in, 2) instantly noting her cyanosis and hypotension, 3) remembering that *Register-Guard* article, 4) quickly diagnosing impending shock, 5) immediately placing a subclavian line to begin treatment with fluids and vasopressors, 6) receiving a rapid response from the internal medicine physician on call, and 7) instantly moving the patient to an open bed in the ICU.

Had I not come upon that article on toxic shock, I may not have suspected the gravity of her underlying condition and the lives of the women it was taking. This was not just impending shock, friend; it was a life-threatening shock caused by a little-known but deadly disease without an apparent etiology. Would my motivation have been as intentional without that knowledge, and the night moved forward as well as it did? I hope so, but know for certain that article put me in overdrive.

Was the Lord, who knows the beginning from the end, working covertly throughout this emergency? I will always believe He was the primary healer and deliverer of a Kiss from Heaven that night and acting like the Savior we know Him to be. Was this a serial divine intervention in the affairs of men, a miracle? From the morning I read that article on toxic shock onward, that I will always believe.

Kisses from Heaven in the Killing Fields of Hell (1979–1980)

I n the late spring of 1979, I noticed something of a drawing in my spirit; it felt as if God was pulling me to Himself. This unusual sense grew until, in my mind's eye, I saw myself settled at the foot of the cross, waiting upon the Lord, and holding on for dear life. Autumn was fading when all of Madison Avenue was preparing us for the Christmas holidays. I was too busy with work to think about it.

Then, one evening over the nightly news came an urgent plea: The United Nations was seeking medical professionals to staff refugee camps built to accommodate thousands of Cambodians pouring over their western border into Thailand. That broadcast, I knew, was speaking directly to me.

Vietnamese armed forces, emphasized the news anchor, were making their way from the east through Cambodia, determined to restrain Khmer Rouge communist Cambodian insurrectionists, led by the soon-to-be infamous Pol Pot, from inflicting further brutal atrocities upon the Cambodian nationalist people.

This extremist, a communist revolutionary leader—driven by a peculiar ideology espousing a lifestyle influenced by the teachings of the French philosopher Rousseau curiously blended with a traditional Marxist ideology—had taken Cambodia from a secure, economically sound, and politically stable society into frank chaos. By systematically winning the hearts of uneducated rural farmers with his propaganda, based partially on America's bombing of eastern Cambodia during the Vietnam conflict, Pol Pot conscripted a large populist army (thousands of whom were preteens) that had gradually swallowed up the entire country in a rule of terror.

In 1975, with poorly motivated Cambodian Nationalist Army in disarray, larger cities were the last to fall. When defenses about Phnom Penh, the country's capital, finally collapsed, pickup trucks filled with child rebels armed with AK-47 assault rifles saturated urban areas, razing, looting, and executing people at random to instill paralyzing fear among the citizenries. True to his purely agrarian philosophy, Pol Pot ordered his troops to eradicate the educated elements of urban society.

Systematically, the overcoming communist hordes slaughtered government workers, businesspeople, students, teachers, and professionals until the streets ran red. These victimized groups marked as "intellectuals"—often identified by wearing eyeglasses (i.e., a sign of education and an ability to read)—were aggressively tracked down like animals and murdered. By most estimates, the Khmer Rouge erased over two million Cambodian nationals in an ideological cleansing of "intellectuals," along with added political, ethnic, and religious undesirables (including Buddhists, Muslims, and a martyred 90 percent of Cambodia's 10,000 Christians).

During this horror, tens of thousands of these citizen "enemies" fled the cities to unsuccessfully seek safety in rural areas while the invaders furiously set about uncovering any remaining city dwellers to herd them like animals into that same countryside. (The Khmer Rouge broadcast lies that the Americans were about to bomb again, this time the capital city to frighten the population into leaving.) Then, with cities emptied and vast areas of once-unpopulated Cambodia settled by the now-enslaved nationalists, the aggressors forced their prisoners to work on labor teams in what eventually became known as the infamous killing fields. Those strictly agricultural projects were commonly under the local control of child supervisors with supreme power over the lives of any worker, adult, or child who complained or contributed less than their fair share of work.

The superiors in charge required other children to watch executions of "uncooperative" adults and their own "disobedient" peers to reinforce the system's strict code of fear-based conduct. To save ammunition, the communists chose death by using pickaxes or suffocation by placing plastic bags over victims' heads. The brutal, unorthodox, and inhumane treatments by Pol Pot's reign of terror kept his captive workforce in rigid submission.

Another Change of Venue

In 1978, when Vietnam's forces crossed Cambodia's eastern border to quell the barbarism in the killing fields, periodic border incursions by the Khmer Rouge into Vietnam territory, and replace the rebel Cambodian government, the undermanned and inadequately trained but heavily armed Khmer Rouge troops fled into western mountains before the far more powerful invaders. Incursion by the Vietnamese soon presented a unique but dangerous opportunity for those trapped as forced laborers in the killing fields to likewise take the same path. Soon, both those fearing the Khmer Rouge along with the Khmer Rouge themselves were joined in a mass exodus, a common flight to cross the Cardamom Mountain range bordering Thailand teeming with its own treacherous set of dangers. The nationalists, already weakened by starvation and severe abuse from the killing fields, became victims of tropical diseases such as malaria, dengue and typhoid fevers, an array of parasitic infestations, and, over time, advanced malnutrition (kwashiorkor or marasmus). Compounding this peril was the threat of encountering Khmer Rouge troops along the way, which meant certain death. Finally, the under-supplied Khmer Rouge, while continuing to furiously hunt the nationalists, faced an ever-present reality as prey for Vietnamese closing rapidly in pursuit. By the end of December 1979, fledgling border camps in Thailand, hastily established by various national, religious, and humanitarian organizations from the world's community, were swarming with desperately ill Cambodians. The refugees initially succumbed at upwards of sixty victims per day as collateral damage from their killing fields experiences, mountain journeys, staggering wounds from war trauma, parasitic infestations, tropical diseases, and malnutrition, which often left those who finally reached safety without enough reserve to conquer death. Only the resolute, back-breaking joint work by those Christian and secular organizations under the oversight of the United Nations—who had for years shamefully refused to heed Australia's pleas to intervene in the ongoing Cambodian carnage—and their reluctant host Thailand eventually altered the downhill course of this holocaust.

Sa Kaeo, a Temporary Holding Facility

An overwhelming need for medical staff in the burgeoning Thailand camps caused a dam to burst in my heart as an immediate inner witness to join this effort. Then I heard Holy Spirit speak: "Go, I have something to show you." It was time to vacate my wait at the cross. Within two weeks, toward the end of the Christmas holidays and halfway around the world, we found our Northwest Medical Team aboard a large, noisy bus overflowing with enthusiastic international relief workers rattling its way from Bangkok toward the border separating Thailand from Cambodia.

Sa Kaeo, our destination, was a temporary facility spread over eleven acres of dry rice patties surrounded by an unscalable eight feet of chain link metal fence crowned with concertina to restrain forty-two thousand communist Khmer Rouge assassins, a scattering of their families, and unfortunate nationalists caught in their midst. The former was not an army; it was an uncivilized mob of murderers, rapists, and brainwashed child barbarians who had consumed Pol Pot's Kool-Aid, fled with tails between their legs before the approaching Vietnamese, and were now under the watchful eyes of disgruntled Thai troops overflowing with disgust for their unwelcome intruders.

Over time, the United Nations workers continued to cull out nationalist hostages trapped within the camp. Despite their successful flight from the killing fields, the nationalists continued to face vicious persecution and death from their communist overlords in the camp, captors who remained ruthless, vengeful, and hardened to human suffering. Implausibly and known to but few, both China and the United States were supplying arms to the Khmer Rouge elsewhere to discourage any further incursion by the Vietnamese in their spreading of communism across Thailand south into the Malaysian Peninsula.

Our Northwest Medical Team served under the cover of World Vision International from a spacious rectangular tent boasting eighty beds and, upon our arrival, fully occupied by the gravely ill. For weeks, scores of new patients lined up on litters outside the tent in the hot sun, awaiting admission. Joining each physician was an interpreter, a bilingual, educated medical, or other designated intellectual who had successfully fled Cambodia in a common struggle to survive.

A Magnum Idea but a Small Caliber Response

Two weeks into our tour of duty came a "magnum idea," a grand solution to a dilemma consuming our Christian hearts for days: How could our team share Jesus with the confined population in the camp? Here we were shoulder to shoulder with forty-two thousand refugees, where few, if any, knew Christ. They were a harvest field begging for laborers, a white harvest field of dispirited, miserable, traumatized, inhumane, and wicked humanity needing Jesus and His grand salvation. And here we were at the ready, with a plethora of Christian workers ready and willing to witness. What about interpreters? More than we could use in a lifetime!

Israel staffed the emergency facility directly across the "street" (a dirt path), while the Japanese orthopedic clinic and prosthetic lab were to our right. To the left were the Christian and Missionary Alliance (CAMA) faithful, who sent nightly reconnaissance teams into the mountains in search of refugees still struggling for safety. The CAMA also supplied the only "professional" Christian in the camp, an elderly Southern Baptist pastor. How, I wondered, could one lone man share the good news with forty-two thousand souls? More motivated than ever, I was determined to take our magnum idea to that pastor for his quick endorsement and implementation.

One morning after rounds, I slipped from our tent to meet Pastor, a delightful silvered-haired gentleman in his midseventies. Twenty years a missionary to Cambodia, he had fled the Khmer Rouge to shepherd a church in Georgia, only to take a recent leave of absence when asked to return to the refugee camps. As we spoke, my spirit soared; of all men, this pastor would have a heart for the interred Cambodians to meet Jesus. He had seen the opportunity, returned to Cambodia to take advantage of it, and would undoubtedly support a concerted effort to evangelize the camp. So, with his permission, I outlined the strategy. Carefully detailing how to overlay the camp with a grid to assign teams to different sections, I enthusiastically pressed on by assuring him there were ample volunteer evangelists and interpreters. Wasn't it exciting? What a possibility! Systematically reaching all forty-two thousand of our camp's refugees with the gospel would be like taking candy from a baby.

The pastor seemed pensive; I waited. Then he spoke: "Let's pray about it." Over the next millisecond, I felt every ounce of air rush out of my enormously overinflated evangelical balloon. "Well," I stammered in disbelief, "may I—may I get back to you in a few days?"

Pastor smiled. "Certainly," he replied as I left, stumbling back to work, deflated and confused.

It made no sense. I even found myself a little ticked at the man for minimizing this outstanding opportunity. Come on, what was there to pray about? Undone but not defeated, I purposed to wait a week and then return to revisit the subject. When I did, Pastor's attitude was unchanged. In my mind, his unwavering reluctance was simply how he chose not to deal with the issue.

Undeterred and knowing that the pastor and his wife probed the depths of the secure camp each afternoon to interact with the refugees, I asked for a time to tag along. When they welcomed the opportunity, I was a little surprised but a whole bunch delighted. For me, this visit into the bowels of Khmer Rouge's stronghold would be an intentional mission, a reconnaissance of sorts. That persistent evangelical dream was not dead; it was merely on hold. Still looking for a breakthrough, this doctor was thoroughly intent on taking full advantage of a once-in-a-lifetime opportunity.

Rescuing "Charlie"

One sweltering Wednesday afternoon, the pastor, his wife, and I set out to negotiate the narrow-cluttered serpentine pathways winding throughout the city overflowing with thousands of blue tarpaulins perched on stakes three to four feet above ground to serve as temporary shelters. Stopping to face one of those low-slung structures—an unusually spacious tent assembled by joining multiple blue tarps into one, I estimated, exceeding one thousand square feet.

Pastor dropped to his knees, only to disappear under the low-slung shelter's roof while his wife and I followed blindly in single file. The following sight was unnerving: packed in rigid rows were over two hundred iron-faced men in black pajamas sitting motionless, cross-legged, and focused on a small vacant area to the front of the tent. As I crawled forward to occupy that space, those menacing black-pajama-clad thugs triggered unwelcome memories of the tour

I had spent in Vietnam years before. No argument from this man; "Charlie"[2] was still alive and well on planet Earth.

Pastor wasted little time presenting the gospel by using colorful cardboard illustrations, continually bathing them in fluent Cambodian. Other than listening to the lilting melody of that lovely language, I limited myself to evaluating the body language of the Khmer Rouge themselves. How unmoved that restrained group appeared, in every way somber, disinterested, and unresponsive, and what a contrast to Pastor's animated preaching. Finalizing the message, our preacher extended this invitation: "Who here today would choose to accept Christ as Savior?" By that time, Pastor's wife had become my interpreter while I, as today's reincarnation of Thomas the Doubter, mused inwardly, *Lots of luck with this crowd, Pastor.*

Hands shot up. Twenty-four, to be exact. Never for a nanosecond would I have predicted that response. Were Pastor and his wife as stunned? Well, they were facedown and weeping profusely on bare ground.

The Aftermath

Baffled, I was unaware of what prompted my hosts' deep emotional responses. Hoping to gain a measure of insight on our return to the CAMA tent, instead, our trek was in silence. This did not seem a moment for probing questions or casual conversation. Rather, it felt like a time to exercise gratitude and reverence. Even I understood that our King had paid today's little gathering a visit, stealing twenty-four lost souls from the kingdom of darkness. It had been an auspicious and holy moment, the depth of which I had yet to apprehend.

Igniting a Move from Heaven

Only later was I made aware of how world-changing had been that moment beneath the big blue low-slung tarpaulin. Those twenty-four

---

[2] A euphemism for black-shirted Viet Cong warriors during the Vietnam conflict

men clad in black pajamas who gave their lives to Christ equaled twice the number of salvations that the pastor and his wife had seen during their entire previous twenty years of missionary service in Cambodia. That, dear Christian, meant but six souls rescued from perdition per decade of sacrifice and far less than one native Cambodian saved per year. Little wonder the missionaries were so undone.

Historically, what made this recent event groundbreaking? Well, the Cambodian people had always been highly resistant to the gospel. Known as the garden spot of Asia, the country had lived for years in comparative peace and prosperity seldom experienced by other nations in the region. Because of the relative political stability, economic self-sufficiency (three exported rice crops a year), and comfortable familiarity with Eastern religions but periodic governmental suppression of Christianity, a wedge had formed between Christ and the Cambodian culture that overwhelmingly excluded Him.

Understandably, the response to the gospel in that afternoon's meeting had precipitated an unexpected torrent of grateful tears and heartfelt thanksgiving from Pastor and his wife. It had been a monumental breakthrough, not only in their lives as servants of our King but, as we were about to see, an early watershed for Cambodian Christianity.

Igniting a Move on Earth

Two weeks later, Pastor paid me a surprise visit during morning rounds. He apologized for the interruption but wished to be the bearer of good tidings before the news became commonplace. *Wow*, I thought, *what news could ever be commonplace in this, the most uncommon of places?* Pastor paused after spotting my inner self-commentary and then continued. Following our outing under the big blue tarp, he emphasized with perceptible joy something marvelous had come about: To date, over six thousand of the Khmer Rouge (soldiers and families, I later presumed) had given their hearts to Christ throughout the camp.

Again, my inner doubting Thomas was on top of this pronouncement: How could that be? How could Pastor reach six thousand souls in such a brief period? Baffled again at first, I was quickly curious as to why but then even more disappointed that he had not sought our help during that wonderful harvest. Once again reading my thoughts, Pastor happily reported that he had done little. It was God's Holy Spirit sovereignly moving to gather the residents of Sa Kaeo into His family. Pastor had simply been a witness to the ongoing event. This time, I was baffled beyond words.

At the gathering two weeks ago, who among us could have predicted that the Lord would awaken a slumbering Cambodia in exile? Not uninformed me. After a mere six years as a Christian, I had yet to hear of an "awakening." So I needed to get this straight: Following our auspicious meeting where Jesus saved twenty-four under that big blue tarpaulin, was Pastor saying that Holy Spirit had hung around for two weeks to save over six thousand damaged souls within an eleven-acre fenced rice patty?

That possibility eluded me. Even at forty salvations per day, we might have expected six hundred souls saved during that intervening period. Inexplicably, the actual number exceeded that expectation tenfold. But could we explain the discrepancy this way? The camp was so congested that the testimonies from excited, newly born-again believers were within earshot of family members and neighbors following Pastor's gatherings. Does that explain six thousand salvations? Unlikely. If not, then how but by a sovereign move by Holy Spirit delivering His message directly to the heart of each refugee. That meant Pastor was correct; I was baffled again, this time beyond reason.

Akin to any outpouring of the Spirit, as this river of God began its uninhibited flow along the border, the Lord continued to draw more refugees to Himself from other camps. One facility, Khao-I-Dang, with 125,000 nationalist refugees, reported 18,000 salvations during the same two weeks. Nowhere near the end, His move quietly continued—one that eventually saw thousands of new Cambodian Christians either repatriated to their own country or emigrated to other nations over the years to become fresh witnesses for Jesus.

A Sunset

Later the same afternoon, following Pastor's groundbreaking news, I stood taking in the most glorious sunset of my life, one that not only took my breath away but over half of Thailand's western horizon with it. Overshadowing the glory of that glowing natural wonder was the spiritual reality that His Son, the radiance of His glory (Heb. 1:3), at that very moment was shining upon our little camp in person. As I pondered this truth, Jesus gently interrupted my thoughts: "Do you remember when I told you (in Oregon) that I wanted to show you something?" I remembered and said so. "Well," the Lord continued, "I really don't need you, son, but I give you the privilege to walk alongside me as I do my work."

To no surprise, His words triggered a not-too-distant memory, the "magnum idea" and grand scheme to evangelize our camp with Christian volunteers. That memory became further tarnished with thoughts of the frustration I had felt over Pastor's resistance to enthusiastically adopt but, instead, prayerfully consider that magnum idea. It was now obvious that the Lord had worked grace through a patient, praying, and obedient pastor willing to wait upon Him rather than depend on the works of impetuous Christians like me to bring Heaven to Earth.

Basking in the majestic beauty of that setting sun, I continued to ruminate, "Who could have predicted that the Lord would select a couple of elderly, worn out, less-than-successful retired missionary evangelists to unilaterally conduct this awakening when so many multi-talented professionals surrounding those missionaries were ready to share in spreading God's Word? Although I had received recent answers to that question, Holy Spirit nonetheless reminded me of another: "'For My thoughts are not your thoughts, neither are your ways My ways,' declares the Lord" (Isa. 55:8).

Doctrinally, that scripture took on previously unseen truth. Having it dramatically enacted before my eyes made it pure, life-shaking revelation. The whole concept of God coming to a rice patty and lighting a fire in the hearts of the most perniciously depraved humanity the world has ever produced was much to swallow. But for the Lord to anoint those same people with the *dunamis* to help catalyze an awakening was unquestionably beyond my grasp. It was, however, unmistakably not beyond Holy Spirit's merciful, impartial, and redemptive hand. One thing was certain—this entire journey had ended as a lesson heartily received, hopefully learned, happily lived out, and indubitably crowned one unforgettable Kiss from Heaven.

Postscript

Remember when Jesus cried from His cross, singling out the very ones crucifying Him: "Father forgive them; for they do not know what they are doing" (Luke 23:34)? The Lord meant this: Those crucifying Him, sullied by Adam's sin, Satan's lies, and religion's lusts, would never have been enforcers of this world's wicked form of justice had they believed the good news that He was the Son of God, and His mercy was to include them in His kingdom. Might those thoughts have applied equally to the Khmer Rouge? So true.

Then, notice that Jesus did not forgive his torturers but instead pleaded for Father to forgive them for their breaking His law. Here is life-changing truth: Jesus did not need to forgive their sin because He chose not to take offense over it. Why? He understood that his torturers did not know what they were doing—the sin, the gravity of the sin, or the punishment due the sin they were committing.

God does not hold us accountable for what we do not know. He is a God of mercy, not punishing us as we deserve but, instead, giving us grace we do not deserve—forgiveness leading to reconciliation with

Father when we open our hearts to Christ. It was no different for the Khmer Rouge when they were ready, was it? Nor is it for those blinded by sin in our world today. The common denominator and miracle necessary here—enter Holy Spirit, the One who is always ready, more than willing, and well able to open blind eyes to the gospel.

Can we also see why the Lord asks us not only to preach the good news of God's love and acceptance to this world but also to become, as He did, the message itself? Is it too late to learn that fewer find salvation through a message taught within the limits of a building than that same message caught outside its walls? The airways may be full of solid kingdom teaching and preaching available to His established born-again body, the Church, but be aware that it was from the highways and byways like Sa Kaeo that Jesus said to compel the afflicted and needy to enter the kingdom of Heaven (Luke 14:23). When the dust settled in our present story, hadn't Father privileged His patient praying pastor to walk alongside Holy Spirit as He awakened a troubled and divided Cambodia to a unifying gospel while making Pastor's previous twenty years of preparation (cultivation, seed-planting, and watering) worth every moment?

So can we now see how Jesus's great commandment to love empowers His great commission to save? How is that? Well, if we seek Him as our first love (Rev. 2:4), we will surely find Him on His current Sa Kaeo-like mission field, a highway or byway among the sin-soaked, afflicted and needy, poor in spirit, and brokenhearted. When we enter that world, become one with those within it, and live in His love, Jesus usually finds us first. Didn't he say, "To the extent that you did it to one of these brothers of Mine, *even* the least *of them*, you did it to Me" (Matt. 25:40)?

QUESTION: Where is the Kiss from Heaven from this God Story?

ANSWER: Our entire Christian medical team was more than ready with a detailed plan to evangelize the entire eleven acres of forty-two thousand lost Khmer Rouge refugees. But for one elderly pastor—a missionary who, for twenty years of work in Cambodia, showed but twelve salvations for his labor—that plan could soon have been harvesting souls. Instead, as the only official religious leader in the camp, Pastor replied, "Let's pray about it," and merely walked the camp each day to do so. Who could understand that approach? And who was not frustrated by it?

Then, one morning, Pastor stopped by to let us know 6,000 souls in our camp had been saved over two weeks' time. That was a hard pill to swallow without our help and harder to believe when Pastor said he had merely watched it happen. Then he said it was all Holy Spirit's work, and he had done nothing, well, but pray.

The afternoon following that morning's mind-bending news, I was watching the grandest sunset, one-half a horizon consumed by an enormous orange fireball. Overcome by its magnificence, while paradoxically mystified by 6,000 murdering heathen rapists having become blood-bought saints without a soul laying on a finger, the Lord interrupted my moment: "Do you remember being told I had something to share with you?" I responded in the affirmative. "Well, Son," He continued, "I don't really need you but give you the privilege to walk alongside me in my work."

Then came the epiphany: If neither our team's nor the pastor's hands-on labor was needed to see those 6,000 come to Christ, then maybe the Kiss from Heaven in this tale was Holy Spirit moving among a city of some of the most heinous villains to ever inhabit the planet and working His will to "save others, snatching them out of the fire; and on some have mercy with fear, hating even the garment polluted by the flesh" (Jude 1:23).

As His finale, I saw the Lord was saying virtually the same thing by offering me the privilege to walk alongside Him as He worked His will (while keeping my hands at home) as our pastor had tried to communicate to all us Christians from the beginning: "Let's pray about it." Lesson learned, Lord: Hands off, hands up, that the glory go to Him.

Epiphany: Doesn't it appear that the Lord is much less interested in what we do *for* Him as what we do *with* Him? All we "doers of the Word" might want to mull that one over for a time.

A Sojourn to Orcas (1983)

Orcas is the largest in the cluster of San Juan Islands sequestered in Puget Sound, a sprawling body of water helping to carve out the western coast of Washington state. Few places can exhilarate an adventurous heart more than this remote part of our country. Each spring, while savagely whipping up the Sound into a blue fury, the last remnant of winter's wind confronts the challenge of a resolute sun straining to pierce a dirty powder-puffed sky with the promise of summer. Tell me, what other struggle could tease a deeper meaning for life from the primal parts of any man?

It was for this precise reason I would come to Orcas Island on that March Day in 1983. As a solo family doctor, husband, and father in a small Oregon town—and after six years striving to create not only what I considered a family practice pleasing to the Lord but also a public persona blended from the likes of Marcus Welby, *Father Knows Best*, and the Apostle Paul—I had, instead, achieved burnout. Struggling through my midlife transition, trying to find a deeper meaning for life, I had paradoxically earned the name "Dr. Wonderful" from my patients and "Mr. Absent" from my family. Striving and driving for so long but achieving no satisfaction, my personal life lay in such disrepair I wanted to run. That was the very thing I couldn't do.

At a personal impasse early one Thursday morning during office hours, I told my staff I would take five days off, starting as we spoke. After ensuring coverage for our patients, I went home, packed my bag, and headed north. Seven hours later, having completed a voyage from the Seattle docks to the Orcas Island ramp, I disembarked from a giant Washington state ferryboat and settled into the rambling Rosario Resort perched on low-lying cliffs overlooking that tumultuous Puget Sound. Sleeping through that night, unusual with a phone at my bedside, approached a spiritual event.

Following Friday morning's breakfast (and coffee to date yet equaled), I took the short walk to Moran State Park, home to 2,400 feet of Mount Constitution, often shrouded in clouds but infrequently snowcapped that time of year. Exploring the park's thirty miles of trails offered a way to get severely needed exercise while satisfying a longing for well-earned downtime. That morning, I tackled the first trail, stopping only when daylight faded into evening six hours later.

Each of the ensuing four days was full of hiking. Invading the very soul of the park, walking every path, and probing each hidden nook and cranny became an obsession. Despite the ever-present chill of rain and mist, I pressed forward, tenaciously winding through the towering firs glazed with dark green moss and silver lichens. Like thirsty sponges, lush six-foot giant ferns, sprawling luxuriously between those giant evergreens, absorbed any residual light seeping through the canopy overhead, only to shake themselves like springer spaniels fresh from the millpond at the slightest touch. Every breath inhaled carried the earthy perfume of a rain-forested floor as an olfactory delight. Regrettably, I had overcompensated for the piercing wet cold by wearing thermal-lined boots, gloves, and a heavy waterproofed coat. The only blessed remedies for the sauna created by my inapt multilayered wardrobe were the steady streams of rivulets running from my drenched hatless head down a bare neck to mercifully cool whatever anatomy downstream they could reach.

There came a time toward the end of my sojourn when I had

walked the vast majority of Moran Park's needle-cushioned, well-groomed paths. Curiously, during those probing explorations, I occasionally came upon unused and overgrown trails no longer open and all but invisible to the casual hiker. Jumping at the opportunity to blaze these abandoned paths to their destinations had been an adventure, challenging me to connect segments that had long disappeared into the underbrush. Rewarding as it was to unravel these mysteries, I never questioned why the park's caretakers had closed those trails. In time, the focus was on tomorrow, my final day on Orcas, and I intended to make that day an absolute best by unearthing and conquering another of those abandoned pathways and one last memorable adventure.

A Setup

Rosario Resort was well-known as a high-end and popular Puget Sound summer playground. This time of year, however, a good share of its warm-weather patrons had other seasonal interests. It was still snowing in the higher climes of the Northwest, where winter sports were the rage, so, for Washington's outdoor enthusiasts, there were better things to do than to slosh through a dreary Orcas Island rainforest in the wettest season of the year. That, I concluded, was why I had yet to meet another human walking in the park during the entire course of my multi-day walkathon. What were the odds of that? Exceptional and not surprising, considering the inclement weather to date.

Though prepared for my last day, I was unprepared for what was to come. That day's sullen sky was darker and colder than most and peppered with low-lying clouds frantically scurrying to avoid the treetops overhead. Happily, within a couple of hours, I had my wish answered. Lurking in the underbrush, deep in a distant part of the park at the base of 2,400 feet of Mount Constitution, lay an ancient unused trail begging for a second chance. Between the shadows, the gray day, and the primitive, unkempt nature of the trail, I was having a grand struggle keeping it in sight.

Discovering it morphed into countless switchbacks steadily climbing in a predictable pattern up a remote face of the mountain helped me uncover sections when I temporarily "lost" them. The lowest-hanging clouds, now clinging to the ground, would obstruct the trail ahead, further hindering the ascent. As these clouds moved on, so would I. When others took their place, I paused. It was challenging, as I had wished, but a little nerve-racking as I often had to blindly grope my way through the progressively thinning underbrush and increasingly sparse and scattered trees as the climb gradually leveled out. Without warning, those ground-hugging clouds suddenly whited out everything beyond two or three meters, obscuring what few reference points were available. What could happen next? Well, plenty! Within seconds, a furious blizzard trapped and cocooned me in zero visibility.

Progress slowed to a halt at the same moment my heart sped up. I knew all too well this was not a good omen. In the open and encased in bright white, I could see but few inches in any direction and hear only the banshee wind as it battered and burned my face with a barrage of frozen pellets of ice mixed with snow. Immobile, rapidly cooling down, and soon shivering, I zipped my jacket and raised its hood while frantically trying to hold ground against those ferocious gusts. Facing an understandable but unwelcome paradox, I felt both a compelling urge not to move at all, competing with an equal temptation to backtrack toward the safety of the denser forest. Conflicted and engulfed in a sea of white with no reference points, while occupying what I knew to be higher mountainous terrain, moving in any direction appeared a crapshoot. Stay put; I knew that I must stay put.

What seemed an eternity suddenly ended when the white curtain instantly rose without warning to reveal a startling vista that turned my knees to jelly. Ten feet ahead lay a sun-drenched precipice, a cliff plunging hundreds of feet into a forest of gigantic Douglas firs, taking on the size of matchsticks beckoning me from below. Strength sapped, I fell to my belly and, dusting off old but reliable Marine Corps tactics, pulled myself along by my elbows through the slick, freshly fallen snow back to the thickening landscape of the forest.

Reaching shelter, I looked back, astonished. The moment of opportunity, effectively seized, had passed. Blue sky gone, the unseen danger was again lurking behind an obscure veil of chaotic swirling snow. The reason for this trail's closure came as no great surprise, and the thought of furthering its exploration became nothing but chilling. And for chilling, well, I had had enough.

Profusely thanking Jesus, I pulled back my hood and began a mountain descent following earlier tracks where I could, negotiating the switchbacks with ease, and intending that my recent harrowing experience would punctuate the end of my Orcas Island adventure, serving as its exclamation point. Rounding the last turn in the trail, which circled a massive fir, I nearly collided with a young man, the single person I'd come across in the park during my entire stay. We were both so startled by the near miss it took a moment for each to produce a laugh. Abundant apologies and then introductions followed.

Well-educated and in his mid-twenties, he was seeking solace among those grand old-growth firs while his young wife, a cancer patient fighting a losing battle with leukemia, was, as we spoke, undergoing chemotherapy at Oral Robert's City of Faith Medical Center in Tulsa, Oklahoma. He had come to Moran State Park at her insistence because it had been a special place for them to reconnect and spend quality time together.

The young man had endless questions and much emotional pain. After helping him address questions about the nature, course, treatment, and prognosis of his wife's illness as thoroughly as I could, an opportunity arose to offer as much emotional support as time allowed. Then, encouraging him in the love of God and the divine plan of Jesus for his life, we prayed not only for his wife's healing but also for God's peace that passes understanding to guard his heart and mind during the days ahead (Phil. 4:7). Before exchanging goodbyes, I shared my recent experience on the slopes of Mount Constitution and, gratefully, convinced him to exit the park by an alternate route.

Postscript

It was only later that I could see the merciful thumbprints of the Lord all over my sudden trip to Orcas Island. Jesus is so often an eleventh-hour God, isn't He? Right up to its conclusion, this journey seemed a time for refreshing and renewal, a way for me to come home reinvigorated and ready to reassume my work, family, and Christian responsibilities. All those reasons were legitimate and true. But the Lord had an ace up His sleeve, did He not? He brought a severely despondent young man, despairing of life's present meaning, all the way from Tulsa, Oklahoma, with a load of questions and abundant pain to meet an overly busy, burned-out physician from Oregon looking himself for a renewed sense of meaning.

Although it would be presumptive to say how Holy Spirit worked in that young man's life through our brief time of ministry, judging from his countenance and demeanor as we parted, I felt confident that Jesus had touched him with His unfailing love while giving him a renewed, Holy Spirit altered perspective for the tough struggle he was facing. Our divine intercept had to assure him that Jesus was totally on board and attentive to that struggle. Once again, this meeting was a well-needed, gentle reminder that Jesus is always with us, waiting for an opportunity to give our lives significance by inviting us to join Him in His work—if we are willing and open to others needier than ourselves. Once again, the lesson learned was a simple one: If we are struggling, we should go pray for someone suffering. It is certain to put our present situation into perspective.

Puzzling over that day's perilous climb toward the upper reaches of Mount Constitution, I wondered what might have been the outcome had that young man, despairing over the prospect of losing his wife, continued to scale that mountain. Was he preoccupied enough to stumble into tragedy? Did he have the background or presence of mind to manage the danger? Would he have taken that precipice as a crowning opportunity to express and end his grief? What if I had not preceded him up that remote, hidden, abandoned trail that afternoon? What if I had not discovered the peril that lay ahead in time to warn him of it?

Nothing happens by chance in the life of a true believer. Nothing is by mistake; everything is Father filtered. His thoughts are not our thoughts, and His ways, not our ways (Isa. 55:8). Jesus often cloaks His motives in our lives with mundane daily events, their deeper meanings unrecognized as significant pieces of a grand puzzle, clear to Him but hidden from each of us. A simple walk through the woods, a challenging ascent to a weathered height, and a "chance" meeting between two strangers are all easily dismissed as life lived out in the ordinary. Yet lurking silently beneath the unvarnished exterior of it all was the ready hand of a wise and compassionate Father poised to move Heaven and Earth as an opportunity to give two of His precious children Kisses from Heaven.

Incidentally, doesn't this tale at its roots not only exalt the goodness of our God but purposefully sentence the "blasphemy of coincidence" to a long-deserved coffin in the lives of all Christians whose steps are ordered of the Lord?

QUESTION: Where is the Kiss from Heaven from this God Story?

ANSWER: Well, the Lord waited until the eleventh hour again to show Himself as not only patient but pragmatic. Unknown to this frazzled man, Holy Spirit had allotted him five days to prepare for twenty minutes of others-centered ministry. Yet I had been so preoccupied and self-absorbed with my burnout, my future, my private life, and my this and my that up to the moment I ran into the young man (pardon the pun), I would have had little to give, and, therefore, him little to receive had I not been revived by gratitude after deliverance from that harrowing summit storm.

Unaware that my new friend was seeking to weather a storm of his own, I was primed (as was he, I felt certain as we met) to welcome Holy Spirit alongside us with the tailored ministry we each needed. In this God Story, the Kiss from Heaven was a perfect opportunity when both our bruised hearts were ripe for His healing agape love to flow. Who then was ready to give as a minister, and who to receive as a ministry recipient? Why, the both of us. And so there arose a not-so-surprising, blessed *kairos* moment[3] choreographed by our eleventh-hour Lord confirming, as we all know, He is no respecter of persons (Acts 10:34) and, as such, the healer of all who seek Him (Isa. 53:4–5).

---

[3] Kairos is a time when conditions are right for the accomplishment of a crucial action that affects lives (from the Greek for opportunity, season, or fitting time).

The Perfect Storm (1984)

Our team, sequestered in a tiny, picturesque village nestled in the mountains of northern Mindanao, the second largest of the seven thousand Philippine Islands, was awaiting tonight's crusade held by our team on a specially constructed, elevated, and well-lit outdoor platform in the town square, a patch of dirt half the size of a soccer field in the center of the little village itself. Native volunteers had heavily publicized this unprecedented event by distributing leaflets over mountain foot trails to both neighboring and distant settlements during the previous two months. That night, an estimated 2,000 curious natives, who had trekked miles over multiple days, flooded the village square. Many had never seen a white face, attended a crusade, knew much of the church, or had heard the gospel message preached. Yet here they were, brimming with Pepsodent smiles and full of expectancy rarely seen in stateside meetings.

To introduce such a throng of Filipino natives to Jesus during our balmy evening crusades, our large bus (one of several)—every square inch a sardine can packed with forty people (Filipino pastors, wives, and five Americans) and supplies to support us for six weeks—spent each day doggedly crisscrossing this dangerous province to the reach that night's crusade. Let me illustrate "dangerous."

Forty-five minutes after beginning the first day's journey, we happened upon local police and the Philippine army investigating a commercial bus overturned on a rural mountain road littered with corpses of the New People's Army (NPA) guerrillas. Those communist insurrectionists had been actively ambushing and murdering a busload of innocents (some I feared still trapped, wounded, or dead within that disabled vehicle) as an act of terror when they themselves were suddenly set upon by Philippine infantry closing after days of hot pursuit.

Stumbling upon this bloody massacre was a sober reminder the territory the Lord had sent us to evangelize was under the control of those vicious NPA rebels who killed mindlessly, opportunistically, indiscriminately, and without provocation to instill terror as an effective way to control the behavior of the surrounding population. We were, without question, in harm's way.

To alleviate our concerns, the Filipino pastors traveling with us had long before emphatically pledged themselves as human shields to protect their American brothers if assaulted. Honestly, revealing their intentions, honorable as they were, did little to build anyone's confidence or allay our anxiety in the least. Rather, if such end-stage preparations were necessary, they painted a threat much greater than any American on our mission expected or wanted to consider as a day-to-day reality. Yet it was what it was.

That afternoon, we found the mayor's home in a little hamlet of two hundred people. Two of us spread out sleeping bags in the living room while the remaining three, including myself, found refuge on the basement floor. All of us could have slept outside as easily, considering we were in the middle of the islands' dry season. To no surprise, nights had been short-sleeved-shirt weather under star-studded skies since our arrival. That evening was no exception as we made a short trek toward the village square, ushered by perfumed breezes wafting through a chorus line of brilliantly blooming bushes lining our winding downhill path to a small city of humanity brimming with anticipation.

Ascending the platform to a vast sea of beautiful smiling brown faces bidding us a warm welcome, there was electricity, an eagerness for the glorious moments that Holy Spirit was promising. Amazingly, this heavily unsaved gathering seemed more than ready to hear from Jesus; in my mind, that was ample proof the Lord had impressed Himself upon hungry hearts even before worship began. It was exhilarating to consider what was to come. Could life be any sweeter?

A Heightened Sense of Dread

Those tender thoughts were short-lived. In the length of a single heartbeat, my eyes riveted upon scores of rifle barrels, reflecting tiny shards from surrounding floodlights and rudely piercing the heavens above the packed throng. Glorious expectancy quickly gave way to a heightened sense of dread; what was going on, and who were those armed men? Were these the feared NPA rebels whose vile work we had stumbled across following that recent murderous ambush?

If not, then who? At once, I set out to reconnoiter our position and to search out the most expedient avenue for escape and evasion. Although it had been fifteen years since leaving my Marine Corps unit in Vietnam, it was easy to recognize the potential for this situation to quickly deteriorate; clearly, we were all sitting ducks on that platform. Regrettably, there was little to do but wait, watch, and pray.

As worship ended, our evangelist shared the gospel to a spellbound audience. In no way was this crowd resisting the Spirit but instead expressing an escalating hunger to know Jesus. To no surprise, at the close of the message, countless folks answered the invitation and came forward to make Jesus Lord and Savior of their lives. Then, within minutes, an added tsunami of Filipinos rushed toward the elevated platform with the evangelist's promise of prayer for healing.

Despite the intense glory of the moment, those rifle barrels continued their threatening presence.

Raindrops Are Falling on My Head

As our team slipped off the front of the platform and plunged into the jubilant throng hungry for prayer, there erupted a sudden, unexpected event: it rained. No warning. No thunder. No lightning. Now, it not only rained, but a gentle downfall quickly became a monsoon-like torrent. Within seconds, we were standing in ankle-deep water that continued to rise to mid-calf. The downpour, perfumed with ozone and warmer than an early morning shower, soaked us all to the skin, baptizing us, it seemed, in liquid glory. Here, in a drier season of the year, came a waterfall from Heaven, obscuring anything outside a radius of a dozen feet.

Caught up in the otherworldliness of this moment, in the melodious praise music, the worshipful abandonment to the Lord, the baptism of a latter-day rain, and Filipinos by the hundreds looking for and finding a touch from Jesus was, beyond all things, a mystical moment as the presence of God fell to anoint His people.

Without hesitation, Jesus began to heal and deliver hundreds of deliriously drenched natives. Countless and repeated shouts of joy and gratitude rang out as people ran here and there between little pockets of commotion to view or show others healing miracles as they occurred. Then a goiter disappeared right in front of me. It was simply too good to be true, and my human spirit found it impossible to fathom the splendor of it all. Beyond question, it was Holy Spirit answering prayer during a supernatural encounter with the kingdom of Heaven.

Then, following an hour of prayer, laying on of hands, and countless miracles, without warning, the music stopped and, spontaneously as it had begun, the deluge ended as the meeting began to dissolve. It was as if angels had closed the spigots from Heaven on their way out of town. Then, in an instant, and as if uninterrupted, a galaxy of stars returned to glisten their way across a cloudless Philippine sky.

Clearing Up a Conundrum

We were all out of our collective minds ecstatic on our return to the mayor's home. What a glorious afterglow! Looking back, we could still see the joyously drenched natives reluctantly dispersing from the town square. Then, the present reality hit. Where were those ominous rifle barrels? Not one was in sight, and, believe you me, I looked carefully and thoroughly. As unsettled as I was about those weapons during the service, I was now equally focused on their absence afterward. Heightened concern now challenged recent ecstasy. What a bizarre but real paradox. During the meeting, we had known where to find "Charlie." Plaguing me on the way back to our quarters was this question: Just where was Charlie now?

A Sunrise Surprise

Waking early the next morning, after tossing and turning the night away on that hard concrete basement floor (sharing it with puddles that had snuck in and drowned my trusty little Olympus 35mm camera during the previous evening's gully washer), I rolled over to see daylight pouring through a small window high on the cellar's wall. Visible through it was a black combat boot bloused with an olive drab utility trouser leg. Dressing quickly, I stumbled my way up the basement stairs. The mayor's house was rising as I glanced out the front door, thankful to see heavily armed Philippine army troops stationed about the perimeter of the property. They were on alert. Ah, palpable relief. Better they were here than the bad guys.

Later that day, a story unfolded: The countless rifle barrels that had pieced the dark sky during last night's crusade belonged to these same Philippine infantry soldiers. The army assigned these troops to protect us during the meeting after intelligence reported that the

NPA communist rebels were preparing to launch an ambush to kill or kidnap the Americans during last night's crusade. That ambush was thwarted, but how?

The conditions had been ideal for a sneak attack on that clearest of nights as our team stood visible and vulnerable on the platform. Despite the Philippine army scattered among the crowd as a deterrent, losing life may have been enormous had the communists executed their battle plan. But Father had a plan of His own, finding a way where there seemed to be no way. On that clear, warm, cloudless, tropical night, Jesus, Master meteorologist of Heaven and Earth, fashioned an instant and prolonged cloudburst so dense that it would obscure us from any would-be communist aggressors for nearly an hour. You could not kill or kidnap what you could not see. So, under the capable hands of our Captain, Holy Spirit, the crusade sailed gloriously toward its fitting conclusion unchallenged, uninterrupted, and tucked safely away from "Charlie" by an opaque veil of Heaven-sent water. The Lord's will done, He spared every fearfully and wonderfully made human from harm's way.

Postscript

The Bible tells us that God holds us in the palm of His hand (Isa. 49:16). Does that mean that Holy Spirit will hide defenseless Christians from menacing others, walking them through life-threatening circumstances to not only avoid calamity but guarantee safety? The nonfiction book *The Heavenly Man* chronicles the biography of Brother Yun, a Chinese Christian repeatedly imprisoned and tortured for his faith. Prison guards had broken his legs less than two months earlier. One morning, Holy Spirit made it clear to Yun in three ways he must escape his Chinese captors at once. Obediently, he left his cell, its door inexplicably left ajar in the prison's maximum-security wing. Then, approaching the first secure gate, another prisoner passing through from the opposite direction opened it for Yun while the guard on duty was distracted by a phone call. Descending a set of stairs, Yun slipped through a second gate unchallenged by a guard who looked directly at him but took no action. Entering the prison's wide-open courtyard through a final door, normally staffed by two sentries who were both absent, Yun limped painfully through the exposed outdoor courtyard to the main entrance and a larger gate likewise left unattended and ajar. Reaching the street—and as if planned to the split second—a taxi took him to the home of a surprised but delighted friend. No one in history had ever escaped that Chinese prison.[4]

Hadn't an angel awakened the Apostle Peter, chained and sleeping between two soldiers, to lead him past two sentries to have a similar experience? "And when they had passed the first and second guard, they came to the iron gate that leads into the city, which opened for them by itself; and they went out and went along one street; and immediately the angel departed from him" (Acts 12:10). Peter in the care of an angel made such an improbable escape from a high-security prison that, when arriving at his safe house, nobody would believe it was him.

In our case, the Lord blinded the eyes of our enemy-in-waiting by a monsoon-like opaque veil of unseasonably heavy downpour until we were safely out of harm's way. Not being a scriptural purist in the arena of miraculous escapes, I have hesitated to quibble about how God limited the vision of our adversaries on that clearest of nights but am simply grateful that He did: "The Lord will fight for you while you keep silent" (Ex.14:14). I'm sure you'll agree this creative miracle, poured forth (pardon the pun) from the goodness of our God's redemptive heart, unequivocally qualified as a Kiss from Heaven—and a wet one at that.

---

[4] Brother Yun, *The Heavenly Man* (Grand Rapids, MI: Kregel Publications, 2002), 48–58.

QUESTION: Where is the Kiss from Heaven from this God Story?

ANSWER: Fresh from the morning's transit through a tragic body-strewn scene following a deadly terrorist attack on a bus-load of civilians by the NPA communist insurrectionists (who met a similar swift fate during an immediate counterattack by Philippine troops), we were instantly put on guard that evening by a multitude of threatening rifle barrels piercing the night air above a large gathering in the public square. Our team and thousands of innocents in the crowd were extremely vulnerable to attack. Whether friendly or not, those rifles revealed an unknown danger, later confirmed as a plan to kidnap or kill the Americans present.

Then, out of a clear sky came a deluge, a tsunami of rain in a dry season, where line of sight was reduced to a few feet, so identifying any specific participants in the meeting from afar became impossible. So the Lord, knowing the beginning from the end, protected His people (saved and unsaved alike) with a blinding curtain of water while, unknown at the time, the Philippine army was acting to repulse confused "blind leading the blind" attempts by the NPA troops to breach the government's perimeter during the rain. That heroic defense ensured our glorious meeting would soon end safely, boasting many salvations and countless healings under our victorious Commander in Chief's star-studded sky.

Any question in identifying the Kiss from Heaven in this God Story?

Thought not. Thank you, Father. Great is Your faithfulness.

12

Healings in Cebu City (1984)

With bodies fatigued and emotions frayed from conducting weeks of crusades in the jungle villages of mountainous northern Mindanao (second largest of the Philippine Islands), our evangelical team was worn out and more than ready for some R&R. Mind you, it had been a glorious and productive adventure, but if you picture us grinding our way through the steamy reaches of that lushest of tropical islands as akin to cruising lightheartedly through the Smokies in a Toyota Four Runner, dear Christian, you have another picture to paint.

Even for the Filipinos aboard, this was roughing it. Rocking and rolling over unimproved trails—designed more for foot and animal traffic than the big buses that carried our contingent of five Americans and forty Filipino native pastors, wives, and workers—we inched our days from tiny village to tiny village to spend evenings introducing those hungry for Jesus and His gospel. None of us complained or even much mentioned the lack of amenities, the frequent mystery meals leading to Montezuma's revenge, threats of malaria, or even the real encounters with the New People's Army, communist rebels who sought our lives and were hell-bent on sabotaging our evangelical outreach. Why no complaints? Because the Lord had brought a vast number of natives into a saving relationship with Jesus while keeping our entire crew cocooned from ever-present threats.

Descending the mountains to enjoy a brief respite in Cebu City, a large population center on the southern tip of the island of Luzon, we happened upon a Tennessee evangelist holding meetings over the next two evenings. While a couple of our team begged off, pegging that venture as a "busman's holiday," three of us considered being spectators without responsibility appealing; we could simply relax and receive well-earned and needed ministry ourselves.

Settling in five rows from the rear entrance of a large, noisy convention center brimming with the excitement of over 2,000 locals, we were quickly charged by the crowd's own electricity. However, "settling in" became problematic as the evangelist's wife, frantically fighting her way through the milling crowd from the platform, pled for us to join her already depleted and understaffed team. We were in the Philippines, and Filipinos commonly expect visiting ministers to pray for believers by the laying on of hands following each meeting. Doing the math, each member of her team would face the improbable task of ministering to over 600 believers that evening; if we agreed, that amount would shrink by hundreds. How could we refuse them in their time of trouble?

As we made our way to a row of straight-back chairs lining the far reaches of the platform, the evangelist had begun to carefully explain the Word of God. At the end, he received an encouraging response to an invitation to meet Christ and followed it by opening the meeting for prayer. The people instantly surged forward row upon row, like Waikiki surf breaking toward the platform. Taking this as our cue, we helpers slid off the stage and were quickly submerged in a tsunami of humanity.

Unlike people of industrialized nations, citizens of the less-developed world are more likely to have "faith to move mountains." That makes sense. Poor and disadvantaged inner-city dwellers—like their native cousins we left behind in the highlands of Mindanao—have little, if any, medical care to take for granted.

Understandably, having faith for supernatural physical healing becomes a defining difference between our two Christian cultures. The availability of medical professionals (physicians, nurses, and ancillary staff) and medical facilities (clinics and hospitals) tempts Western civilization to depend less on God's supernatural intervention and more on man's modern medical prowess.

In other less prosperous parts of our world, however, patients have often never seen a doctor or visited a clinic. Offered no alternatives, they depend upon Holy Spirit (as they know and understand His ministry) or other spiritual entities like Shamans (witchdoctors) if they have not yet met the Lord. Supernatural healing among these poverty-stricken natives is not a rarity. Yet, despite having recently seen and heard a variety of people claim such healing on our journey, I remained a skeptic; my scientifically trained mind had yet to wrap itself around something so intangible.

An Ambivalent Path

At twelve years old, I announced my intention to become a physician. It was a well-thought-out but not terribly forthright decision. Give me grace, please—I was twelve. Idolizing our family doctor (and my dad's fishing partner), both my folks believed there was no higher calling than to become a doctor of medicine. Yet there I was, a young boy with a peculiar habit of rescuing every sick or wounded four-legged or two-winged critter hobbling down life's critter-risky highway as ready targets for my fledgling veterinary skills. Deep in my heart and from my earliest childhood, I harbored a desire to become a veterinarian, a vocational choice that had unspoken potential to create significant disappointment in my nuclear family.

Was I to pursue a career as a medical doctor or in veterinary medicine? Not yet thirteen years of age, it had not escaped me that capitulating to my parents' wishes would reduce their incessant dwelling upon my future, which felt distinctly like arm-twisting to their son but good parenting to them. Rightly, at least as I perceived it as a preteen, I saw medical school light-years away, and by evading my folks' unsolicited encouragement during the intervening period, I might have a finite chance to preserve my mental health. Succinctly, all that parental "encouragement" drove me bonkers. Contemporaneously, it did not escape my devious little mind that reaping the rewards of parental pride that would go with "my son is going to be a doctor" would also have a colossal upside. So, given the appearance of acquiescing to my parents' heartfelt desire, I wrote my seventh-grade term paper on the subject, "My Vocation: Medicine," while—steadfastly and silently, I must confess—continuing to covet my dream of becoming a veterinarian. Never recognizing the enormous degree of long-term satisfaction my misleading ways might encourage my folks nor how deeply my less-than-transparent childhood declaration would penetrate their hearts as irrevocable truth, I went about my suddenly more or less uncluttered life as a usual teenager.

Then and before we all knew it, college, military service, marriage, and children had become my cluttered life as an adult. Regrettably, my ever-present vocational dilemma had not changed one scintilla. Believe it or not, it had been sixteen years since that "convenient decision" to schmooze my folks to gain temporary relief by a less-than-heartfelt (okay, less-than-truthful) commitment. So should it have surprised me, as I was now pushing thirty, that my parents still held fast to their dream of medical school while I had not forsaken fantasizing over veterinary college? No.

Conflicted as ever, I applied, from the jungles of Vietnam, no less, to both institutions of higher medical learning to allow my conundrum all the freedom needed to solve itself. Clever chess, don't you think? True, until receiving acceptances from both the Veterinary College at Cornell and the State University of New York's Upstate College of Medicine. So much for any career as a counselor of conflict resolution. Then, after a long and serpiginous journey, the solution was even more bizarre: Cornell called for a nine-month wait, but I would start medical school at Upstate within three. For our GI Bill to kick in required enrollment in about any school; having little income or savings and three children to feed, the decision became painfully adult. The parents were ecstatic, I more resigned, and my dog, I sensed, overly relieved.

Entangled in the Scientific Art of Medicine

The first two years of medical school were purely lecture and lab, with the last two immersed in a clinical setting. Applying the knowledge learned in a classroom to real-life practice in a hospital setting dominated the life of a medical student. By the time I received my degree, I was inexorably indoctrinated by and in the scientific reality of the art of medicine (scientific art: somewhat of an oxymoron, don't you think?). Here is a quick gist: every medical disease or condition has a tangible cause that may be scientifically determined or at the least potentially understood, and, if correctly diagnosed and treated with proper therapy, will result in at least measurable healing or restoration of normal physiology and function.

As you can see, this approach, endorsed by any critical thinker, leaves little room for a concept of miraculous intervention. The supernatural (otherworldly or inexplicable by the scientific method or critical thinking) cannot be part of medicine's healing equation. Believing otherwise, I was told, belongs to the world of the ignorant, unenlightened, uneducated, and the religious.

Praying in Unbelief

Praying for all those hungry Filipinos took over an hour. It was a heartwarming experience to move among hundreds of expectant believers, impatient to exercise their faith and receive from Jesus. This was a new experience for me; praying for people at home, I admit, could be tedious, empty of faith, and unrewarding. It did not help to know that a smattering of these folks would call my office for an appointment in the morning after God had inexplicably passed them by the night before. It was always the same: I became their default but necessary healer. That never felt valid and generated a little too much pressure if I thought about it. So I didn't.

That night, the first person upon whom I laid hands was an elderly woman somewhere in her late eighties. Confined to a wheelchair for three years, she was beyond blessed by the prayer, which blessed me to no end. At least something, I mused, would come from this, even if only to bring comfort and joy to an old woman with an alleged back problem. Various folks that evening had a laundry list of requests, while the rest trusted that Holy Spirit would guide our prayer. *Whatever works*, I thought. Unabashedly, I prayed that night out of respect for our evangelist's wishes and the heartfelt desire of all those Filipino believers for prayer. The truth: I had little faith for anything to happen. I did not believe for a minute that prayer could heal in this setting but that its advantage was to emotionally comfort and share God's compassion with the recipient. That had been my day-to-day Christian experience and seemed ample enough reason to spend time in this activity.

Was I disappointed at the absence of any instantaneous physical healing taking place in the lives of those for whom I prayed? That would have indicated an expectation. Look, I did not expect a thing because my scientific grid would not allow it. Believe in the supernatural all you want, but healing "miracles," given enough investigation, were always subject to pure, unadulterated logic and scientific truth.

Disputable Evidence

The following evening, our contingent of ministers entered the platform to find the Tennessee evangelist encouraging Christians to come forward to honor the Lord for healing them during the previous night's session. Another wave of Filipinos responded, waiting patiently for their tum to testify. From the platform's furthest shadows, I found myself focused on one aisle where an elderly woman was shuffling her way from its darker recesses. I recognized this old woman, even without her wheelchair, as the first person for whom I prayed the night before. She was glowing and waving to the cheering crowd every step of her way to the platform.

Reaching the evangelist, she testified of being wheelchair-bound for three years due to back pain, but during last night's prayer, God healed her back, and she no longer needed the chair. The audience clapped madly as she returned to her seat, waving as she went. I thought, *Well, she is old but surely not that disabled. Old backs? Don't I know old backs! Good one day, bad the next. Anyway, this event has given her a little notoriety and extra attention; isn't it amazing what people will do for a little time in the spotlight? Secondary gain in the elderly is an amazing psychological blessing.*

The evangelist, now taking his second testimony from someone I did not recognize, did not steal my focus from the old woman shuffling back to her seat. That her wheelchair was nowhere in sight did not escape me. What also struck me was the third Filipino now testifying was another upon whom I had laid hands, a fourteen-year-old boy suffering from severe asthma from birth. The increased AP (anterior/posterior) diameter of his chest (a profound distance between the breastbone and the spine, which is a sign of significant chronic pulmonary disease) and wheezing last night had revealed respiratory illness. Tonight, he projected his voice and breathed with no effort while claiming God had healed his lungs.

Well, I reasoned, *we know that the diagnosis of asthma has multiple causes and exacerbating factors; there may have been changes in his disease by reduced stress levels, favorable weather variation, a reduction in today's pollen count, or proper administration of his medications. Who knows?* All I did know was another thing as unpredictable as a bad back was chronic asthma. As I reached that clinical conclusion, the evangelist turned to an excited man in his forties, more than ready to share his story. Surprised I was, as you too might be, to recognize him as another of the folks for whom I had prayed.

Out of curiosity, I moved toward the front of the platform. This Filipino gentleman was in the bold process of informing the crowd that after long years of severe prostate disease, he was urinating normally. In his exuberance, no one could deny this man was convinced that God had touched him. Conceding that for any adult Filipino male to testify before 2,000 mostly female attendees he was peeing like a baby was a reasonable sign that something significant had happened at last night's meeting. After all, we all know that Filipinos are often modest folks.

Indisputable Evidence

At that probing moment, a scene unfolding deep down the aisle in the far reaches of the building interrupted my thoughts but captured my attention. What I saw prompted me to finish the remaining few feet to the platform's edge. Skipping up that center aisle were two young sisters, one ten and the other fourteen. The elder was a healthy teenager, while her younger sister, for whom I had prayed, was born deaf and dumb. She could not hear, nor had she ever heard or spoken with any clarity. She was mute. The evangelist questioned the older sister as to why she and her sister seemed so effervescent. "What happened?" he asked. With visible joy, the elder girl spoke, "My sister could not hear and could not easily speak. Now, after last night's prayer, she hears and speaks."

The evangelist, extending the microphone, turned to the little girl and said, "Say, 'Praise the Lord.'"

She repeated, clearly, "Praise the Lord."

The evangelist, rubbing his thumb and forefinger in front of the little girl's ears, one after the other, questioned her again, "Do you hear the same from each ear?"

The little girl shook her head, showing she heard from one ear more clearly than its twin. The evangelist put his fingertip in the bad ear, prayed, and then retested her hearing. Hearing in both ears was now the same to the little girl. The whole healing thing destabilized my thoughts and left me dumbstruck.

With the entire arena now delirious with praise, the sisters briskly returned to the twilight in the rear of the building. Then, with all eyes but mine focused on the evangelist listening to the final testimony of the evening, I watched those two sisters as they joyfully hugged and kissed one another. As a finale, they erupted in laughter and dance, holding each other's hands while twirling around and around and around in pure ecstasy for minutes on end.

Postscript

In retrospect, it seemed obvious to some why Jesus chose four of six healing testimonies (that, mind you, is still too small a cohort for an adequate scientific study) from folks with whom I had prayed: "You have the gift of healing."

"More likely, I suffered unbelief and needed convincing," was my response when offered that observation. Remember, I earlier entertained plausible diagnostic opinions formed from two of my early "brief medical evaluations," was more drawn to another as a conundrum, and only saw the mute girl's change as scientifically inexplicable. It was clear from my examination the previous night that the little sister was mute. Tonight, it was obvious she was no longer mute. (However, even eyewitness testimony in a courtroom is scientifically suspect.) In my mind, even if the evangelist's evaluation was the most convincing argument for this girl's healing, the most compelling was what happened in the far recesses of the building that night. The genuine joy of those sisters—freely given in dance, song, laughter, and worship that only the most biased, rigid, and close-minded person could deny as heartfelt truth and honest declaration—held this assurance for me: Jesus had supernaturally healed that little girl.

The scientific method leaves little wiggle room for deciding truth by subjective testimony, while in faith, subjective testimony is a lynchpin of belief. As a clinician, I base my medical decisions and practice on facts mostly gleaned from and supported by objective investigation and conclusions reached through histories, various examinations, large, well-documented research studies, and other supporting information, data, principles, treatments, and proven cures. As a man of faith, I base my life on the Bible (*Logos* word), application of the Bible by Holy Spirit (*Rhema* word), His subjective leading, testimonies that confirm others' experiences or mine, and faith that does not deny true science but may go beyond it.

Science is never meant to answer the unanswerable (until possible according to its own method), and although allowed to lay out possibilities (theories), they may never be considered truth until scientifically proven. When science presents theories and calls them truth, like evolution, for example, then it has betrayed its own rigid standards for veracity and has moved into faith. This faith is not based on Christian determinants for belief but on reaching beyond limited scientific investigation into incomplete documentation, unproven principles, political correctness, or woke ideology.

Evolution is not scientific truth, however, although it might be part of it. The scientific community, often desperately driven to find a degree of preferred truth in life, may stretch the borders of documented theory, construct an altered reality, or even promote fiction to find it for a variety of ideological reasons.

Hitler had "proof," you remember, of Aryan superiority, while former Vice President Gore and his attack on well-chronicled cycles of global climate fluctuations (which no one denies and was recently confirmed again by finding tropical remnants in the seabed off Antarctica) has coerced climate science from a place of elegance and truth to frank prostitution over the billions to be made by turning green politics into greenbacks. Taxing sinister CO_2 molecules to keep our planet green when those CO_2 molecules are the reason it is green? Really? Yet what better way for a one-world government to homogenously fleece every human pocketbook than to measure carbon output by measuring the CO_2 you exhale 24/7 with monitors (or later imbedded chips)? Outlandish? With the recent Covid experience, we are halfway there, duped and manipulated by exalted talking heads, puppets preaching unvalidated pseudoscience as intractable truth, the blind leading the blind into the pit, and calling it a marvelous feat as many profited, more died as a result, and many more shamefully looked away.

One hypocrisy (heresy perhaps) of modern-day religion has become its subtle incorporation of the spirit of the scientific method to support the Bible and the doctrines of faith. Can you see how the culture has affected the Church by insisting on strict rational approaches to supernatural (now considered irrational) events? Little wonder parts of the Church have dissected the Bible free of most otherworldly testimony and left it lifeless, a joint (structure) with no marrow (life). Again, look at the Jesus Seminar, a half-truth.[5]

While science has resorted to undocumented faith (theory), faith has moved toward depending on documented science. In both cases, the dilution has been to the disadvantage of each's purity. Science has moved toward fantasy (look at choosing one's sex or mathematics satisfied with nearness of truth). Then, faith has moved on to prove itself by archaeological, astronomical, or biological facts. Come on, who can scientifically substantiate the Red Sea parting, a dinner for 5,000 men

---

[5] The Jesus Seminar was a group of mainline biblical scholars throughout the 1980s and 1990s that excluded from the Bible over 80 percent of the words spoken by Jesus and characterized Him as a prophet-sage who told parables and made pithy comments, etc. (John Dart, *Los Angeles Times*, March 4, 1991).

plus families catered by Jesus and a little boy with two fish and five loaves, or Jesus Himself taking evening strolls on the Sea of Tiberias?

Anyway, I am getting way over my own opinionated gray head. And, trust me, all the above is opinion until proven truth by the scientific method or certified as biblical fact. Here is the point: All my preconceived assumptions and conclusions about healing—well-documented and scientifically valid, grounded and based on rational thought—had been correct but limited by the bias of the scientific method. And don't you know that I was more than glad to be found out? I was ecstatic. A whole new joyous world had suddenly opened beyond my world of science; it was the world of faith. By the goodness of God, I had stumbled over my own scientific ideology and fallen headlong into supernatural reality ("they will lay hands on the sick, and they will recover" (Mark 16:18) of the ignorant, unenlightened, uneducated, and the religious—and, I might add, an enormous Kiss from Heaven.

QUESTION: Where is the Kiss from Heaven from this God Story?

ANSWER: It is easy to join the rush to point out that little mute girl or the entire pack of four folks for whom I prayed who received supernatural healing that night as our Kiss from Heaven here. Do so with my blessings and support if you choose. Let the rest of us focus elsewhere. Are you able to see that American medicine and much of the American church share a common significant bias against supernatural healing, even when such healing is a common event in both medicine and religion among poverty-stricken nations? The next question must discover the common denominator in that shared bias when we find it impossible to deny supernatural healing except by hiding behind either the scientific method or the traditions of men. Finding that common denominator is simple: It is Jesus Christ.

Why does acknowledging Jesus as healer become difficult? Well, if you acknowledge supernatural acts, you must acknowledge a supernatural actor. Then, if we acknowledge Him and His power to heal, we are next legitimately forced to recognize and honor Him as God and lose our control as the prime movers in medicine, the Church, and our own lives. So when we deny Him on Earth, He denies us in Heaven. This takes secular humanity way beyond what it is willing to consider in any depth.

It is easier to be dishonest and simply manufacture and adhere to a bias like the scientific method and the traditions of men. But when we do, in the end, we are confronted with Romans 1:20–25; 28–32, which must be attacked, cursed, and ignored as nonsense for the fear those scriptures are true and, if so, apply to all humankind and, finally, reveal a very poor prognosis for one's afterlife.

So what has all this to do with being a Kiss from Heaven in this God Story?

Perhaps not a lot directly. But indirectly, if you don't believe that little mute girl was healed by Jesus, your Kiss from Heaven may yet, though paradoxically, rest in taking a hard look, in an opposite spirit, and responding in an adequate way to all those passages from Romans.

However, I suggest, not before attempting to get a good night's sleep.

Milford's Chinese Dinner (1985)

Milford was a legend in his own time, at least to others. Never had I heard, let alone seen, the man myself. Don't they say that seeing is believing? Well, do not count on it, dear Christian; there is an exception to every rule. Decked out in a broad-collared World War II vintage brown-and-cream-checkered wool sports coat that hung to his knees and draped in a necktie as wide as Manhattan, here was this old bowlegged guy dancing and strumming his signature ukulele to "Victory in Jesus" while singing up a Tiny Tim falsetto storm to set our Sunday night service in motion. Trying to find a seat, I stood frozen in a pew, blocking folks behind from the surreal sight in front. Listening to Milford's warbling, which caused his unsecured upper plate to rise and fall like a little hand clapping in perfect rhythm to the music, the only thing lacking from this vaudeville act was a "straight man" with a cigar. George Burns, where have you gone? Allow this, I will: Milford lent authenticity to what it meant for God to have a peculiar people. Until that moment, I had seen no Bible verse used with such understatement as I beheld that night.

Milford was a well-known prophet, the church's pastor announced. That was a stretch. Fish-eyed behind smudged Coke-bottle lenses, strings of thinned-out hair flipping about, he continued to merrily prance to his own music around the platform. Occasionally

spewing little showers of spittle from a well-hidden reservoir sequestered above those uppers, he could have easily met the description
of a Barnum and Bailey runaway. But wasn't it supposed to be the
other way around? Didn't people run away to the circus? Texas was
Milford's home, but tonight, he was in Cottage Grove, Oregon, visiting
old friends who were both my friends and patients. Not seeing them
in the congregation told this story before it even began.

After announcements, Pastor turned the meeting over to Milford,
eager to share a little and then much. He was a Canadian who began his ministry flying an old, rickety seaplane each Sunday to the
Niagara River above the falls. There, after setting an anchor to keep a
beach full of sun worshippers within earshot, he and his ukulele (or
a violin by older reports) would climb onto a pontoon and preach an
hour of the gospel. Over the years, his unique personality made him
an object of everything from fascination to scorn, but his prophetic
gift kept him in demand. As silly as this old guy appeared, his word
carried authority, and his command of Scripture held your attention.

What finally won anyone over during an encounter with Milford
was not so much his eccentricity as his genuine love for his fellow
man. Wasn't it predictably like the Lord to anoint such a guy to promi-
nence? His prophecies that night accurately "read the mail" of a dozen
Christians in the crowd. He concluded his extended time of ministry by
gleefully sharing he had an invitation to China, a lifelong dream from
years of prayer. He also made it plain he, seventy-eight, could not go
meandering halfway around the world alone. Would the church pray
for someone to go with him? Everyone enthusiastically agreed to his
request, though none, I noted with interest, came forward to fulfill it.

Rumbling over the Main Street railroad tracks on my way home,
I reviewed Milford's evening antics. It was difficult to admit that the
old geezer had quickly grown on me. As crazy as the whole night had
begun, by the end, he was without question God's man. The proof of
the pudding, says the elderly proverb, is in the eating. Although, in

Milford's case, it was more like fruit salad. Then, settled back onto the smooth asphalt, the Lord spoke to my spirit, "I want you to take Milford to China." Oh my, I wanted nothing of the direction this exchange was heading, none of it.

"No way, Jose," I heard myself foolishly respond. Predictably and patiently, Holy Spirit repeated Himself. Not good. History had shown that instruction that needed a third time from Jesus was never a charm, nor anywhere near charming. Obedience and two weeks in Asia were a much wiser choice. "Okay, Lord," I squealed like a stuck pig in tune with my tires U-turning their way back toward the church, "I'm your babysitter."

The prophet was still jabbering away to a captivated crowd and enjoying every minute of it. Milford, if you have not already noticed, loved to talk—and talk incessantly. When able to get a word in edgewise, I asked for a moment, and he consented. Within seconds of volunteering my "babysitting" services (for all he knew, I might have been a serial killer), he enthusiastically accepted. Our China adventure had begun. Oh my, had I only known.

Leaving the meeting, I wondered how my family would respond. Memory of an earlier mission trip to a far-east refugee camp—where a nasty tropical disease had hospitalized me in a five-day coma—had understandably led to questions about my priorities. After all, I was our breadwinner. Tonight's disclosure would rekindle those concerns. To complicate things, my wife struggled with the very concept of hearing from God, although clear with what Jesus said: "My sheep hear My voice" (John 10:27). Forthright as it is, this scripture had become not just a point of contention in our family but also for various factions of the Church, at least until a personal encounter with Holy Spirit confirmed it. Strong opposing opinions surrounding the subject of hearing from God was something that I had learned to grudgingly accept, but if my orders from headquarters tonight were Heaven-sent, the Lord had clearly not.

A Chinese Fire Drill

Two weeks later, in a Hong Kong YMCA, Milford and I met to develop our trip's strategy. Helped by his longtime missionary friend, expelled from China by Chairman Mao along with countless other Western missionaries in the late forties, we set out to smuggle Bibles across the border from Hong Kong into what was then Canton. This effort, planned out to the last jot and tittle, went down in flames as the Chinese border guards, using newly adapted fluoroscopy, scanned, discovered, and impounded our precious cargo. The 1980s were not times to dally with the communists at the border. Smuggling unlawful contraband was an offense worthy of prison.

Then, in police custody, another side of Milford appeared, one which we instantly came to appreciate. Approaching the Chinese border guards detaining our prophet, he changed into a man bold as a lion and shrewd as a serpent. As if portraying a slice lifted from the life of David acting out before the King of Gath (1 Sam. 21:13), Milford (minus the drooling, as I recall) went gesticulating from one Chinese authority to another while systematically pleading our case with mindless ramblings in his deep Texas drawl. Eventually, this blatantly bizarre behavior confused and seemed to intimidate our captors. None understood a word from Milford but quickly lost interest in devoting any more time to this loony-tune American, either in or out of jail. Within minutes, sans Bibles, the guards released us to cross the border. Everyone understood what we had seen: It was Milford under another anointing, a level beyond what I had seen in Cottage Grove. Holy Spirit could shift gears in the old guy like nothing I had ever seen.

Within days, we lodged at the only English-speaking hotel in Kunming, a large city to the west northwest of Hong Kong, which opened to Westerners within the previous thirty days. It was a bustling metropolis found at the northern tip of the magnificent twenty-four-mile-long Dianchi Lake teeming with enormous wooden junks busily engaged in commerce. Bordering the lake to the west, there loomed an imposing sheer cliff punctuated with caves, the Dragon's Gate Grottoes, housing Buddhist temples and various cottage industries. The cliff, accessed by a path carved into its rock face, ascended hundreds of feet from the valley floor and lakebed. Milford carved out his own reputation on that rock face during our journey. I have not the time nor the willingness to live vicariously through this babysitter's PTSD moments involving that cliff incident again. Later, after therapy. Maybe.

Indigenous Chinese, raised from childhood to hate Westerners, were still wearing the blue uniforms of Mao's failed Cultural Revolution, disciples banned to this area years before when the supreme leader's movement to purge all remnants of capitalist and traditional elements from Chinese society fell into calamity. One-half the population continued to wear those high-collared uniforms while the rest wore more contemporary dress styles or those of the Chinese army. It seemed customary practice to refuse service to Westerners in local stores, but this rebuke paled in offense to irate Chinese citizens angrily confronting us by jumping up and down on sidewalks, waving their fingers in our faces while screaming profanities. Since no one could understand our English, we would respond to the public's hostility by patiently listening to all the unintelligible rantings designed to mock and disgrace us by adopting affirming body language and smiles. Whether this made inroads was unclear and, to this day, only known to the Lord Himself. Any unrest we presently have with China understandably has significant roots. What we appreciated in all the chaos was our "City of Refuge," a hotel removed from the heaviest part of the city where we found safety from earlier public vitriol by dining evenings in the hotel's restaurant. A satisfying meal, warm fellowship, and a little civility with decorum were a guarantee to soothe away any of our day's emotional goose eggs.

The Chicken Missile

Seated in a near-circular red leather booth in the hotel's dining room one evening, our threesome was busily enjoying quasi-American cuisine while reviewing our trip to date. Credit any ambiance in the room that night to low-intensity ceiling lights casting a dull incandescence and creating broad shadows over our table. Milford, to my right and directly across from his old friend, was struggling to find the next bite in the twilight of his plate. Spending the time listening intently as the two old comrades shared the glory days of Christian evangelism in China, I imagined missions organizations reaching into the heartland of this primitive country to establish outreaches among simple cultures that one by one opened their arms to Christ. These stories made my heart hungry to hear more long after my belly was satisfied.

Milford was in the middle of one of his tales, his voice ebbing and flowing in rhythm with those annoying uppers that refused to know their place. Squalls of rice, like snow flurries swept in by a Northeaster, rushed from his mouth to randomly scatter themselves across the table. Like a highway ever so slowly obscured by an unrelenting blizzard, the tabletop threatened to lose such low-lying landmarks as napkins and coasters if this onslaught continued. It became increasingly difficult to separate his friend's head movements as encouraging nods of affirmation for Milford's stories from maneuvers to evade those incoming mini rice mortar rounds.

While the prophet spoke, he was also looking to insert small pieces of boneless chicken into his mouth at strategic intervals. At one point, his right hand, wildly gesticulating in ever-widening arcs above his head to emphasize a point of conversation, held a piece of chicken tenuously grasped by the prongs of an uncertain dinner fork. Slipping the surly bonds of Earth following a carelessly executed high-gravity maneuver by the fork, the morsel of chicken, now a short-range missile rocketing to an apex of eight feet, plunged swiftly back to Earth behind the backrest of our booth. Now, mine was the only vantage point suitable to appreciate the entire melodramatic scene that followed.

Abutting the back of our booth was one of identical proportions occupied by two adult Chinese couples. Nicely dressed and obviously privileged, they were happily eating their meals when the incoming "chicken missile" struck the dead center of one gentleman's dinner plate. Plop! Oh my! At impact, he lurched backward in his seat and, gathering his wits, earnestly scanned the room to ferret out the source of attack. Despite a systematic survey of his surroundings, the action had been so covert and sudden that his only recourse was to notify his tablemates of their jeopardy and encourage them to search for the source.

By this time, I was struggling so hard with laughter within that a little slipped out, so much so I took a moment to compose myself. Milford, interrupted from sharing a colorful story by my short-lived outbreak, had a quizzical look on his face, head tipped to the side and forward not dissimilar to that of a puzzled Labrador retriever. "The piece of chicken on your fork," I began, struggling to maintain my composure, which unintentionally baited him, "it flew off and landed on the plate of the Chinese gentleman directly behind you."

As I stated my case by not withholding the gravity, Milford's eyes widened. The longer he looked at his barren fork, which spoke volumes, the more the Labrador's curiosity peaked. "You beggar," he countered with uncertainty; Milford called everyone a "beggar" when puzzled or questioning another party's intention.

"No sir, it landed dead center in the middle of his plate," I continued, "that's why everyone behind you is scanning the area and talking so intensely." Nodding toward the Chinese couples to emphasize my point prompted Milford to look over his shoulder, where he instantly recognized the full gravitas of the moment. With mounting trepidation, I accurately read the look that crossed the prophet's face;

somehow, he had precipitated an international incident, which was his duty before God and man to settle. Without a word, he moved swiftly to his right, exited the booth, rounded its corner, and made a beeline to bring clarity and resolution to this sudden turn of world events.

Now, you already understand that Milford's appearance always demanded considerable emotional latitude from those unaccustomed to his unconventional retro dress, flappity-uppers, hurricane hair, and wild-eyed-Coke-bottle-magnified intensity. So, as you might expect, his abrupt, uninvited intervention into that vigilant but ill-prepared party of Chinese innocents ignited pandemonium. This time, four people lurched backward, every face etched with various levels of surprise, unbelief, or frank terror. Then, Milford, sprinkled generously with rice and oblivious to the impact of his chaotic appearance and behavior on these gasping folks, bent over at the waist to draw face-to-face with the victim of his chicken missile. With a voice raised to a controlled shout to guarantee clarity, he boomed time after time in agonizingly slow but meticulously enunciated Texan: "AHHH AAIM SOOO SORREE THAAAT MAAA CHEEKENNN FELLL OONNN YOOORR PLAAYTTTE!"[6]

All Milford's decibel-laden, detailed, long-winded, and carefully crafted words fell on Chinese ears that had absolutely no understanding of why this crazy, round-eyed, rice-covered American was hovering over their table, let alone why he was bellowing like a wounded water buffalo. Those folks could not understand one word of Texan. (Laurel and Hardy, eat your hearts out.)

Then, assignment complete, Ambassador Milford, hastily and with a restored air of dignity, returned to home base, gratified with his successful mission to avoid the impending international crisis. At the exact moment he proudly and confidently relayed these assertions, his recently detained but now liberated Chinese victims, still wide-eyed and in one level or another of psychic shock, hastily gathered

---

[6] "I am so sorry my chicken fell on your plate."

their belongings to compete in an all-out "outta my way" sprint to the nearest exit. Upon leaving, we noticed those folks left sizable portions of authentic Chinese food on every plate, including one occupied by one poorly skewered piece of quasiAmerican chicken.

Putting a lid on that evening, Milford finished his celebration by spewing another salvo of (now cold) mini rice mortars across the great divide with his old friend. Not one of us could stomach (a poor choice of words) sitting through that day's craziness again. But who could predict tomorrow with Milford in command? The Bible says this about the Lord's experiences, "And there are also many other things that Jesus did, which if they were written in detail, I suppose that even the world itself would not contain the books which were written" (John 21:25). Want to know something? You might confidently say that Milford was running a close second.

Postscript

God has a peculiar people with His man Milford in the lead. At one time, I wondered if he were from a different planet; could that have been the planet Goofy? On second thought, that would be Pluto, sadly kicked out of our solar system's kennel within the past year. Would I make it to Oregon without hernia surgery after laughing so hard and often? What was so disconcerting? The old guy was more often serious as a heart attack. When we finally hit Hong Kong on the way home, Milford had "gigs" scheduled in the local churches. So he tuned his uke, donned the WWII gear, and we hit the circuit.

The welcome and honor the prophet received made me simultaneously jubilant and ashamed. Here were throngs of honest, intelligent, and well-healed serious Chinese Christians overjoyed with his arrival and deeply respectful of his ministry. Yet the man had not changed an iota but was still the "real meal deal," entirely authentic Milford. That made me wonder if God was not putting the squeeze on me for looking at this guy as a quasi-demented old goofball. (Oh, don't you know I still loved him like a grandpa?) After nights of prophetic impartation to hundreds of almost-swooning Chinese (Chinese and swooning is another oxymoron, yes?), I had to repent again for not appreciating and honoring the prophet's gifts and profound anointing.

Learning God's ways (which are not ours, I reminded myself) during those remaining days with Milford Kirkpatrick caused me to undergo an overdue attitude adjustment. Few of the slick, charismatic preachers, highly educated teachers, and devoted missionaries with whom I was familiar held a candle to this one man's gifting. It dawned on me it took real character for him to carry such a level of anointing without hurting others or puffing himself up. God's safety net for Milford was his self-effacing humility, love for everyone he met, and willingness to be a fool for Jesus.

Feeling like a stuffed shirt, a constant dripping from a corner of his roof, and now undoubtedly ashamed by how I had subtly tolerated the old man during our journey, I had to repent with godly remorse. The lesson learned was a pearl of great price: Just what we do means less than who we are in Jesus and the latitude we give Holy Spirit in ministry. Jesus said, "Apart from Me you can do nothing (John 15:5)." All the fluff and pizzazz mean nothing in a ministry unless it is Jesus's fluff and pizzazz. Somehow, that does not jive with His own self-evaluation, "for I am gentle and humble in heart" (Matt. 11:29).

Years later, when the Lord told Emily and me we had the "ministry of lasts," I knew not only from where that came but also felt honored to be tucked away into that little pocketbook. It meant that Jesus could easily have his way with us, that we were pocket change, easy to reach, nobodies with little to offer or lose, and no challenge to His Spirit. Anything we did without Him, although it might occasionally amount to "something" among men on Earth, would ultimately be nothing before the throne of Heaven. What we did with Him as our prime mover through us, however, would produce fruit, please Father, and bring Him both glory and honor (John 15:5).

One fine morning, I awoke to this thought: *When I grow up (in the Lord), I want to be like Milford.*[7] *Forget the flappity-uppers, the ukulele, and the retro dress, Jesus; all I really wish is the old man's tender heart, his simplicity, transparency, and, for certain, his anointing.* To be forthright, it has been a long time waiting for an answer to that prayer and getting longer by the day.

Realistically, this may be one Kiss from Heaven this old man may have to reluctantly forgo.

---

[7] Milford Kirkpatrick (1912–2002) was a principal participant present at the origin of the Latter-Day Rain Revival in North Battleford, Saskatchewan, Canada in 1947. He was a humble man who spoke little of himself, a whole lot about the Lord, never anything of being a force in that earlier revival or throughout the movement following. It was thirty-five years after our trip to China that I researched this astonishing man of God's life. Of this we may be certain: Milford will still be casting crowns when we meet again.

QUESTION: Where is the Kiss from Heaven from this God Story?

ANSWER: What is in a name? In the name of Jesus, "God of Salvation," is everything the Lord is and, therefore, everything He does as our glorious God of Heaven and Earth. Defining the name Milford literally, "wading across the river down by the mill," defies explanation that encompassed everything Milford Kirkpatrick was and did. From that first Cottage Grove moment to our China goodbyes, he was as unchangeably unique in his ways as Jesus was in His.

We all have but a handful of people God has blunder-busted across our lives to make a point. Milford was one in mine. To this world, Milford was a silly old geezer; in God's kingdom, he was a titan. When I spent time to understand what it takes to end up such a man, it became abundantly clear that no Christian reaches such a pinnacle in life unless chosen, set aside, and anointed by the Lord. There is little chance for us becoming a Milford Kirkpatrick. No offense, friend, but when the Lord put that man together, He threw away the mold.

Have you ever been brought low in the presence of a goofball who considered the Lord everything, himself of no account, and those around him as opportunities to lay down his life while never thinking or saying so but simply being and doing so? In all his apparent audacity, Milford never noticed himself—never. Only others. He embarrassed my Christianity, caused me humiliation for my thoughts and behavior, in deep need of repentance, and left all my life's trophies in a heap. That was my Kiss from Heaven found in this God Story. I will never get over that life's lesson . . . and never hope to.

Understand now? No? Well, maybe you needed to be there. I could have used the help.

The Romanian Roadblock (1991)

The violent overthrow, kangaroo military tribunal, and execution of the iron-fisted Romanian dictator Nicolae Ceausescu on Christmas Day 1989 opened the doors of this former Soviet satellite to the hearts and hands of the entire planet. Aid and volunteer workers from faith-based and humanitarian organizations flooded the country, helping to bring stability to its fledgling new government. Orphanages crammed with malnourished and inadequately housed and dressed children quickly and understandably became media focal points for the relief efforts. Less reported was a rural agricultural population ecstatic over the dismantled and abandoned communist agrarian collective system, consisting of innumerable enormous farm complexes of white-washed buildings, farm equipment, and vast acres of tillable soil. Deserted by thousands of formerly conscripted but newly freed citizen laborers, these collectives lay as ghost towns dotting the countryside. The churches, no longer targets of alleged philosophical resistance or harbors of potential political rebellion, once again overflowed with hungry believers still unsure of their newfound freedom to worship without persecution.

Regrettably, there persisted a force—rarely visible but more threatening than produced by the behemoth cloud erupting from the 1986 Chernobyl nuclear plant meltdown, which had rained harmful radioactive fallout throughout this land and a healthy share of the Earth. This malevolence was covertly working throughout Romania to threaten the very fabric of the country's fledgling democracy.

The Chernobyl Meltdown

The Chernobyl nuclear plant meltdown was not as much an unexpected disaster as it had been an unaddressed fear. The world knew of the Soviet's lack of resources, caution, and expertise with their nuclear power plants. Unfortunately, there appeared no political way to access and help that Russian bear who tended to secret away every faux pas, failure, and frank disaster she experienced from the world's community.

Miraculously, when the reactor exploded during a routine maintenance check conducted by insufficiently trained workers (but may have been gross negligence by the engineering staff), only 3 to 5 percent of the nuclear core was involved. That was enough to kill twenty-eight people acutely and later a fistful of others. Four thousand extra cases of childhood and adolescent thyroid cancer (gratefully curable) arose among six hundred thousand people exposed to elevated levels of accumulated radiation. Blood dyscrasias, like leukemia, expected to rise dramatically, fortunately did not. The ensuing cloud of yellow radioactive debris overshadowed a great part of Europe and western Asia while concurrently reaching the higher latitudes of eastern North America. It was intriguing to find that a small hospital near the town where we lodged in northern Romania posted a graph illustrating a spiraling increase of spontaneous abortions (miscarriages) for a year after the disaster. Citizens in the town also shared that the following spring's cucumber vines produced blooms but no vegetables.

A Scourge on the Land

Long after the killer cloud from Chernobyl had vanished, another "cloud"—a violent and oppressive remnant of the former Ceausescu rule little recognized by the rest of the world but well-known to all Romanians—continued to cast its cruel shadow over the country. As a poison looking to destroy the renewed spirit of the newly liberated land, the deceased dictator's coveted security forces had surged relentlessly on as vicious, unrestrained terror teams who roamed the land to intimidate its citizenry into continued submission.

For years, Ceausescu had compensated prostitutes working the high-end resorts along the Black Sea to take "work-related" pregnancies to term to supply his orphanages with children destined to become raised and trained as sociopathic killers to form those dreaded terror teams. When on duty and depending on the team leader's pleasure, those unrestrained killers indiscriminately blocked highways, randomly stopped vehicles, interrogated their occupants, and then, on the leader's whim, either murdered or released their victims.

The terror teams left over following the dictator's death were in no measure accountable to the new government. These maverick packs continued to flaunt their brutality, ignoring the newly established rule of Romanian law, and became a severe contraindication to the country's self-portrait as a fledgling democracy to the rest of the world.

We three musketeer evangelists were initially unaware of those terror teams, but not for long.

Touching the Past

We had a scheduled Sunday evening service three hours to the southeast. The trip offered a chance to explore this Rumpelstiltskin-like country, recently awakened to a new world order after tight seclusion as a captive Nazi state before World War II and then an even tighter Soviet satellite thereafter. Despite the eventual demise of the Soviet system, Romania had remained in the hands of its long-term Soviet puppet and recently executed unstable dictator.

This afternoon, in a land reminiscent of rural America in the 1930s, we were bouncing along narrow ribbons of highway through tiny, quietly struggling, rundown rural hamlets. Here and there were dilapidated stores with lonely one-pump gas stations while, fittingly, teams of giant plow horses pulled wagons overflowing with families, goods, and manure through the streets. Droves of tattered people walked alongside the roads while automobiles, when seen, were scarce and elderly. This panorama was in harmony with the hospital we recently visited, one equipped with a heating system limited to the daylight hours, patients lounging in beds while dressed in street clothes, ether as the single general anesthetic, virtually no antibiotics, and a sky-high mortality rate. The medical staff would not allow us in the ICU.

Romania, clearly stopped in its tracks for decades, caused us to wonder how this country could gain any traction to escape its present moribund state or find necessary momentum down the line to do so.

Tense Encounters

Later that evening, we finished our service before a typical Romanian church family who had yet to lay aside the hard but no longer relevant lesson that expressing overt emotion would encourage government agents planted in the congregation to investigate them as religious zealots on Monday morning. While cruising through the pitch-black countryside toward our home base, I continued to silently relive the evening by recalling how those stoic Christians, hard-shell Baptists all, had ended our shared time with grateful tears pouring down their expressionless faces. What a privilege to have seen such living paradoxes as the Lord touched tender hearts beneath those decades-old programmed and protective icy hard exteriors.

The road that night felt unsettling, even eerie; I mentioned so to our driver, George. For an hour, we had not seen a single vehicle approaching from either direction. Then, while entering the outskirts of a sleepy little village, dark except for a dimly lit section of road near its epicenter, there appeared a well-lit checkpoint guarded by Romanian troops in full regalia, weapons at the ready, and official about their business. George, our Romanian expatriate driver, whispered through clenched teeth, "Don't say a thing. Let me handle this!" Fear laced his voice, which automatically jump-started my own hyper-alert state of flight-or-fight readiness. As a United States Marine in Vietnam, I had been here.

Pastor Bob Curry, our companion and team leader, sleeping soundly and spread eagle over the entire backseat, stirred and then sat bolt upright as we faced what now presented as a full-fledged military roadblock. While slowing the Volkswagen minibus, George rolled down the driver's window and, feeling a little flushed, I followed on the passenger's side. Even before coming to an abrupt halt, soldiers obtrusively thrust rifle barrels through our open windows within inches of our chests. Frozen by this unwelcome intrusion, Pastor Bob and I remained motionless while George, a Romanian banished from the country by Ceausescu years before as a political enemy, was already engaged in an intense dialogue with two soldiers.

The tone of their conversation, although I understood none of the language, sounded strained from the outset. As the tension steadily mounted, I could see and feel that something was palpably wrong. Faces, body language, and the tenor of the voices betrayed the direction of the interchange. Without warning, George reached frantically across my chest, forcing one of those freezing and unwelcome steel rifle barrels to cling tenaciously to my exposed neck. Then, in one sweeping effort, he delivered a manila envelope from the glove box directly to a Romanian soldier reaching partway through his window but not before, I hasten to add, that rifle barrel, now tenaciously frozen to my neck, sent me an early warning.

Soon, more guards were busily examining the contents of the envelope, their comments coming faster and more furious by the minute. This precarious situation was escalating, a point clarified by the soldiers becoming weary and increasingly more frustrated with

George's tone and behavior. *Something, Lord,* I thought, *something must change, or this shouting match will demand the soldiers to take decisive action.* Predictably, it did!

A Defining Decision

With no warning, the soldiers rapidly withdrew their weapons while brusquely returning the envelope to George, who slapped it back into the glovebox with fanfare and a sense of finality. Frozen gun barrels gratefully gone—accompanied, I might add, by indeterminate layers of perfectly good skin rudely stolen from my now paradoxically grateful neck—we rolled up the windows, turned up the heat, and rudely left that blockade and its town in a cloud of actual snow and metaphorical dust.

Continuing to take deep, repeated, controlled breaths while wiping his brow in twenty-degree weather, George forced a wobbly smile before beginning his story. Earlier in the evening, one of those malicious terror teams had forced a car to the side of this highway and, before withdrawing, executed two of its passengers. Radio and television stations quickly ordered audiences to vacate all highways while the Romanian army set up checkpoints, one of which confronted us along roads nearest the point of attack. When the soldiers stopped us, they had been on high alert and beyond anxious because the road, long emptied of all vehicles that night, suddenly presented a lone van despite the wide dissemination of that heavy news alert late Sunday evening warning citizens to remain off the highways.

Critically complicating matters, George had left our passports at home base and knew that he could not properly identify us as legally in Romania. He skillfully but deceptively stalled the troops for as long as he could and then, with a desperate move to further hold off the guards, blindly grabbed the Volkswagen Owner's Manual (written in Swedish) from the glove compartment as the only document within reach. The soldiers questioned the owner's manual for an extended period and finally agreed that it was a ruse and by no means an adequate means of identification.

As the military poised to extract us from our vehicle for questioning, George, having had several severely unpleasant experiences with army interrogators in the past and praying desperately to avoid another, heard a deep, commanding Romanian voice from the farthest reaches of the gathering: "Oh, they are just the gospel," boomed the voice, "let them go." That commanding voice of authority propelled the soldiers to swiftly withdraw their weapons and release us. Wow, what in the name of Heaven had happened?

Postscript

Could Rod Serling (Carbon dating myself again, aren't I?) have turned this adventure into any better "Twilight Zone" thriller? Let me say that passing from a sweet Sunday night of worship and ministry into such a perilous and tense encounter, only to enjoy such an incredulous extraction, far exceeded what we could ever have predicted as a finishing touch for that roller coaster of a day. Had we not been about His business, how might this story have ended? Interrogation? Imprisonment? Torture? Disappearance? The military in Romania still had a dictatorship's mentality, the license, and the licentiousness to act without restraint.

The Bible is clear that God is not so unjust as to forget our past or present ministry to His Church (Heb. 6:10). Every angel assigned to us by Heaven that evening must have felt the gravity of our situation. To whom then belonged the deep, authoritative voice that had pierced the frozen night air, interrupting those angry guards on the verge of enforcing decisive interrogation?

How had that voice known our mission when there were no official or valid legal documents to identify us at that tiny village outpost? Who besides we three knew we were the "gospel"? Father knew, and His angels knew. It was indeed a Kiss from Heaven to have someone conveniently join us with unquestionable authority, ready command of the Romanian language, and in our eleventh hour of desperate need.

"George?" you ask. No, not George, Christian. Trust me, George was no angel.

QUESTION: Where is the Kiss from Heaven from this God Story?

ANSWER: In the mid-1980s, on a daily run near our Oregon rural home, I came to a property surrounded by six feet of stone security wall, a peculiar sight in this deep country setting. It took no time to clarify the wall's purpose. A goliath brown and black Rottweiler racing through an unattended gate stopped me in my tracks, blocking the road ahead. Teeth bared, the growling animal, now a tiger hugging the ground, was stalking me and about to make his intentions clear.

Dressed in running shorts and a tank top with no mace or pepper spray to ward off an attack, my only choice would be to intentionally sacrifice a perfectly good left arm as a meager offering and final defense against this monster. All my attempts, from gently talking the animal down to using my command voice, had no impact. Now, six feet away with uncompromising eyes fixed on this foolish interloper, he paused, ready to complete the pitiless task for which he had been trained for years behind those six feet of rock. The adrenaline was flowing through my every pore and, with showtime upon us, suddenly, an authoritative elderly voice slipped over that impenetrable wall, calling that beast by some incongruous love handle, who nonchalantly assumed the form of an obedient poochie and disappeared through the open gate into that rock fortress.

Whether that memory bolted into my awareness as that frozen rifle barrel pressed against my exposed neck as a backdrop to the mounting tension between our driver, George, and those hostile Romanian troops manning that night's barricade, I don't recall. As unidentifiable foreigners with no passports and clearly trying to deceive their captors with false documents, it did not take Sherlock Holmes to see we were in major jeopardy. These troops, generations deep in totalitarian rule enforced by a code of terror, were salivating to interrogate these potential murderers to obtain the truth one way or another. They, like that Rottweiler, were about to happily do what they were trained, and we, like yours truly on that memorable Oregon run, needed somebody with some clout to end this nightmare.

George, an expatriate Romanian familiar to such treatment in the past before banishment from the country by Ceausescu as a political enemy, was sweating profusely in twenty-degree weather as our captors' intentions surfaced.

Understandably, I was having no more trouble believing this whole unbelievable event than when facing that crouching Rottweiler years before.

Suddenly, breaking a palpable silence as the troops were quietly planning their next move, an authoritative voice from behind some metaphorical wall on that dark night suddenly called off the dogs and sent us packing. Then, like the Rottweiler disappearing behind all that rock, those military troops disappeared from our rearview mirror. Curiously, I never saw the dog's caller in Oregon nor the troops' commander in Romania; nevertheless, I knew who to thank. Sometimes, our help in times of trouble, those inexplicable but extraordinary eleventh-hour Kisses from Heaven, are angels unaware if we believe.

And, sometimes, even if we don't. But God.

"Go to Concordia" (1998)

I t was a blustery gray, overcast Missouri afternoon in the spring of 1998. The shoulders of our interstate highway, not yet scrubbed by the spring rains, were camouflaged by last winter's road dirt. A drab and uninteresting time of year to travel, our path offered few signs of new life. Emily and I, having recently left Pensacola, Florida, after six glorious weeks at the Brownsville Revival (Pensacola Outpouring), were heading for Smithton, Missouri, home of another, although smaller, move of God. In contrast to the world about us, we were squeaky clean and bursting with new life and expectation for what awaited us at the Cornfield Revival in Smithton. Brownsville had been beyond what we hoped for but merely whetted our appetites for more to come.

Interstate 70 runs east and west, from St. Louis to Kansas City, across the State of Missouri. Heavily traveled by America's eighteen-wheelers, it had emerged from winter's onslaught penetrated by bone-rattling potholes lying in wait to repeatedly stagger our little motor home. Making matters worse, that day's grayness had later abandoned us to a dark, moonless night, denying the possibility of avoiding the highway's relentless assault on our defenseless little Minnie Winnie. Heralding ultimate surrender to this incessant abuse, with one last blast, our tormented little vehicle's alternator warning light lit up precisely as her high beams dimmed. Uh oh—I knew what had happened.

Exiting the interstate to release the hood, there hung the cast aluminum alternator brace, cracked in half with belt dangling. Within a stone's throw of an exit ramp, we were within minutes sleeping deeply in a nearby motel, awaiting morning and the chance to have our rig repaired. About 3:00 a.m., I awoke curiously refreshed and, looking not to disturb Emily, sought the seclusion of our bathroom to read. Feeling my way across the nightstand to pick up my Bible and glasses, I slid silently along the wall through the ink of the room and past the foot of the bed. While groping for the bathroom door handle, a loud and commanding voice crashed the silence, stunning me and filling the room, "Go to Concordia!" Stopping short, heart pounding, I tried without success to visually pierce the darkness for a human invader, even when I knew in my spirit this was the voice of the Lord. Gathering composure, I recall whispering, "Where would that be, Lord?" No answer was forthcoming, and further reflection on Concordia's whereabouts got me nowhere. So I planned to use our road atlas, packed away in the RV, to search out Concordia's location with first light. As you might recall, internet cell phone GPS availability was a thing of science fiction for we common folk in the late 1990s.

Although shaken but not overcome, I was determined not to miss what God had for us in Concordia, wherever that might be. Drowsy after reading a couple chapters, I returned to bed to fall fast asleep. Looking back, doesn't that response seem profoundly nonchalant for somebody who experienced a personal visit from the God of the universe? Stay tuned; we are merely beginning.

A Change of Plans

Breakfast complete by 10:00 a.m., we were merrily cruising west on I-70 toward our destination, the Cornfield Revival, ever so grateful to the Lord that our recent interruption had been brief and the alternator brace so easily replaced by an auto repair but 100 feet from the motel. Okay, I know what you are thinking: "What about the voice? What about 'Go to Concordia'?" Truthfully, I had forgotten. "Who does such a thing?" you ask. Kind of speaks for itself, doesn't it?

Well, here we were, all hunkered down, "fat, dumb, and happy" (a well-worn aviator phrase indicating a state of complacency and lack of readiness for any unexpected occurrence), when suddenly a small green official interstate roadside sign announced: "Concordia 50 miles." About to lose control of the rig, I cried out, "Concordia," rudely stealing Emily from her morning's devotion. There it was— Concordia, the city to which the audible voice directed us last night. Shaking my head in wonder, I shared the news with a now-attentive Emily, who took this change of venue like doing bacon and eggs instead of oatmeal, searched the atlas, and found our new destination. Shortly, bypassing the Smithton exit, we closed in on Concordia's.

Along the way, I sought the Lord, "Jesus, is there anything we need to know?" Instantly, Holy Spirit spoke these words to my spirit: "No, absolutely, no!" Intuitively, I knew we were to deliver this message with authority; it felt every bit a command, as did last night's authoritative words in the dark or our motel room. Concurrently, I saw those same words as a banner headline (a word picture) across my mind. Whoa, the Lord had serious business to conduct with someone. Pressing Holy Spirit again, I looked for more. A brief but distinct picture (inner vision) of an outside phone booth appeared. Then, nothing.

Asking further of the Lord met with silence. He had spoken. Then I forewarned Emily, "Let's keep our eyes open for busy outside phone booths when we reach town."

Where's Waldo

Concordia, Missouri, was a small rural town of twenty-three hundred people, bordering Interstate 70 and within an hour of Kansas City. It was a clone of Midwestern and Southern farming communities where thriving small businesses yet lined busy downtown streets. Negotiating our way through side-by-side friendly neighborhoods generated fond memories arising from both of our childhoods lived in similar settings.

As delightful as today's journey down life's highway was going, our mission to find an occupied phone booth was not. Oh, there were outside booths scattered throughout Concordia, but not one occupied. That made sense, considering we were in the new age of the cell phone. Crisscrossing the town for upwards of an hour changed nothing, as did waiting in a city park for another while moms strolled by a phone booth with their dogs and children. Becoming exasperated, a little weary, and a bunch bored, we tossed in the towel, pulled up stakes, and headed downtown.

Finding an open princess parking spot directly before a bronze plaque announcing "Concordia, Missouri, Birthplace of Kathryn Kuhlman" caused Emily's heart to leap. As so many Americans, she admired Kathryn as an anointed healing evangelist of the mid-twentieth century. Curious as to whether there might be a museum or library nearby, it took less than five minutes before we were poring over three bulging albums collected by the town's librarian, who, as I recall, had been friendly as a child with Miss Kuhlman. Then, she had gone way beyond her official duties by chronicling media reports, documents, and photographs of Kathryn's entire life. Now, Emily was ecstatic.

Leaving the library full of gratitude to the Lord and His servant librarian who helped us vividly recall the glory days of that great woman of God, we reentered our car to puzzle the day's events. Although the Lord blessed us with that library visit, in my experience, such a blessing is usually followed by fulfillment of Holy Spirit's wishes. But here we were, about to vacate this town with no satisfaction as to why we had come, let alone what the inner vision of a phone booth or the inaudible imperative, "No, absolutely no," meant. Equally confused, we could not help despairing over the failed outcome of our search.

Driving north, we passed the entrance to a service station preceding the onramp to Interstate 70 leading east toward Smithton. Bordering the station's entrance was a phone booth and, next to it, an imposing black Pontiac Trans Am. Exiting a small space atop the driver's side window of that behemoth black car and running to the booth was a receiver cable. Eureka, after four long hours, had our eleventh-hour Holy Spirit reliably snatched His victory from the jaws of our defeat? Time would tell.

Meeting "Jesse"

Braking quickly, we backed the Minnie Winnie through the entrance to the service station and strategically parked her where both the phone booth and the Trans Am were directly in sight. Then, fixing our eyes on this promising scene, we settled down to wait. Emily was quiet. She said nothing. That was fine; I did not want conversation. By the Spirit, I knew we were precisely where the Lord wanted us, despite my pounding heart and everything within me ready to bolt for Smithton. Have you ever noticed, Christian, how the flesh contends with the Spirit at such moments?

A cascade of thoughts rushed to say I was out of my lane or looking for trouble. Despite all those ongoing multiple dark-side objections, I remained entrenched, determined not to miss what God had in store and to see this through. Ten minutes labored on; nothing changed. During that interval, I noticed the Trans Am sported opaque black windows. Who was in that car? What kind of person hides behind opaque black windows? My mind was spinning with crazy questions like this. Fifteen minutes passed without a word from Emily or any activity from the car. Feeling isolated and a little queasy, I knew there was no turning back. Oh, but the enemy kept trying.

Twenty-minutes. Twenty-five minutes. We had been hovering here for a full thirty minutes when a muscular arm penetrated the now open driver's side window, rocketed the receiver into its cradle, and rapidly retreated behind the opaque windows of that big black vehicle.

Out of the motorhome as proverbial greased lightning, I shot thirty feet between the two vehicles, cartwheeling around the driver's side rear fender of that black beauty. "Nuts," I muttered, "that driver's side window is closed tighter than a tick." A mere two feet from an invisible driver beyond that wall of black glass, I was overtly aware that the driver had his gaze locked on me. Tentatively, I knocked on the center of that impervious window. Nothing! Do you know what "nothing" feels like at a time like that? Well, it nearly convinced me to cave and run the "hundred" in nine seconds flat. "What," I asked myself, "are you doing here?"

Suddenly, that black window cracked and began an agonizing descent while little by little revealing the object of this entire day's frenetic search. Suddenly, if ever, it was time for an apoplectic event. Two short feet away, framed in black and glaring directly at me, was this enormously intimidating gigantic hulk of a man, head shaved without a hair and sporting a gold ring in his left ear. Gulping, I thought, *This guy looks like a bigger, scarier version of Jesse Ventura* (if you can imagine that) *or, at best, a really mean Mr. Clean.*

On cue, "Jesse" erupted, rumbling like an ever-ready Vesuvius, "What do YOU want?" Know what? It did not feel like it mattered in the least to this colossus what I wanted. No, not one iota!

Stealing a quick breath, I whined within, "Lord, this is not fun!" Then, hoping Holy Spirit would fill it, I opened my mouth, "Sir, this may seem a bit out of the ordinary," I began, "but would you allow me five minutes of your time?" He grunted and continued the stare. (Tell me, friend, what does it mean when King Kong grunts and stares you down?)

Ignoring the little bit of common sense left but not the opportunity, I pressed carefully forward, rambling on to my newly found friend about how Emily and I had broken down, taken the motel room, heard from the Lord, came to Concordia looking for someone in a phone booth, and, finally, after hours of searching the town came upon him seconds from our departure. No further rumbling, comment, or even a whisper issued from "Jesse Vesuvius." Only the stare. Brazenly interpreting his silence as a willingness to spare my life and hang around for Act Two, I cut to the chase with the Lord's message: "I have no idea what this means, but the Lord says, "No, absolutely, no!"

OK, my mind raced, *my delivery boy's job is over. Let's vamoose.* Stepping back, I took a final look at Jesse. His lower lip was on his lap. He was also a tad gray, or green, or somewhere between. It was hard to tell. "What," the Kong mumbled, "what was that?"

Redelivering the message with a little more command voice but still half an octave high, "The Lord says no, absolutely no," froze Jesse as if smoked by a taser. Unsure his attention was still intact, I pressed on by taking his brief but convenient shock-like state to sum up how I saw my part in this whole matter (as if the man might care): "I don't need to know what this is about, sir. That is between you and the Lord. I'm just a messenger."

Jesse—still looking as if he had been severely dazed by George Foreman's best right hook—now stared straight through me; I could see that the message was shaking him deeply. "No," he pleaded, "please stay; let me tell you what has happened." Then, right before my eyes, this mighty mountain of man became a little molehill of a child, contrite, a trifle afraid, and uncharacteristically confounded.

What, I questioned inwardly, *is going on, Lord?*

Conviction and a Clean Heart

Over the next moments, this broken man humbled himself before God and a perfect stranger, confessing that he had just spent over an hour conversing with a former girlfriend who, coincidentally (ask the devil about "coincidentally," Christian), was en route to conduct business in the identical city as Jesse. During the chitchat, they agreed to meet at a hotel to spend the night. Although Jesse was neighing agreeably with this lusty arrangement, something within him was now having second thoughts (ever consider where "second thoughts" come from?). As we spoke, he admitted to "praying each day" and that there was a "wonderful Christian lady" in his hometown whom he hoped to marry.

By the end of our brief time, the Spirit of God had apprehended, convicted, and then pulled Jesse from the fire (Jude 23) with one simple phrase: "No, absolutely, no!" As his curtain call while closing that black Trans Am's driver's side window to separate us until Heaven, Jesse Vesuvius vowed with renewed confidence, "Before we spoke, I was going to spend tonight with that woman, but now," he paused looking me directly in the eye, "I'm going home." And then Jesse Vesuvius disappeared behind that impervious black glass and drove away.

It Is Well, It Is Well with My Soul

Amazed, even awestruck, I walked pensively back to Emily, who was waiting patiently in our little motor home. Heart bursting with gratitude for the small part we had been privileged to play in today's drama staged by Heaven, and despite my fumbling ways, it was obvious what Holy Spirit wished had come to pass: He had snatched Jesse from the jaws of premeditated sin and saved me from missing God one more time—again. What sweet Kisses from Heaven for all partakers.

Postscript

We live on a tiny planet twirling at 1,000 miles per hour and traveling at 60,000 miles per hour through a pocket-sized solar system consisting of eight planets revolving around a small star. That same solar system is traveling at 480,000 miles per hour roundabout the center of our Milky Way galaxy. Milky Way, 100,000 light-years (six trillion miles per light year) from stem to stern, is traveling at 124 million miles per hour through ninety-six billion stem-to-stern light-years of universe.

Considering the size and scope of things cosmic, any angelic traveler would stumble over the Milky Way as a mere David among Goliaths while trekking among David's estimated two hundred billion mostly larger sibling galaxies in our observable universe, each the home of one hundred billion stars. If we theoretically lumped all galaxies in that observable universe together, astronomers predict there would be two hundred billion trillion stars roaming around within it. That estimate is conservative and limited by yet unavailable technology for deeper space exploration, while the prospect of multiple universes (a multiverse), if true, might increase the number of stars to press infinity. We know this: the preceding mouthful of space knowledge is too much to swallow as a single cosmic big gulp. Swallow we must, for there is more to come.

Now consider this: The Bible tells us the Lord hung those two hundred billion trillion (and counting) stars in space, gave everyone a name (Ps. 147:4), and has simultaneously kept track of each one rocketing its own course through the heavens. If that does not stagger your mind, what about His keeping up with five hundred million newborn stars each day? That is a rate of five thousand star births per second. Mitigating the effort required to keep track of these new additions, there is an identical number of contemporary star deaths. That eases the pressure on those star-counting astronomers but hardly on the Lord, who must find names for each of the five hundred million newborns where countless galaxies are rapidly separating themselves from one another on the one hand or coalescing with their neighbors on the other. Talk about moving parts, numbers, and names of which to keep track.

As if the Lord had not enough to occupy Himself in space, here on Earth, He assigns a number to each hair (Luke 12:7) on every one of this world's two and a half billion Christian heads, which becomes an ever-changing exercise considering that 80 percent of the world's humans will suffer hair loss during their lifetimes. Then, He orders the steps of every saved, righteous saint. Remember, there are two and a half billion blood-bought Christians on this planet, each averaging 7500 steps per day. This means the Lord orders 17,250,000,000,000 (seventeen trillion two hundred fifty billion) steps per twenty-four hours.

Pressing on, let us not forget that He notices every sparrow that falls to the ground (Matt. 10:29). Since the Lord is no respecter of persons (Rom. 2:11), might we consider that His impartiality extends to the remaining 50 to 450 billion of His feathered friends on Earth? That might even require burning midnight oil for the Lord, which is not an issue since He never slumbers or sleeps (Ps. 121:3). Finally, and cutting to the chase, He is out there counting our tears (Ps. 56:8), every spoken word (Matt. 12:36), knowing each name (Rev. 20:15), every soul who fears Him (Mal. 3:16), and every godly work finished (Heb. 6:10). Is it fair to question why I spent hours researching the preceding waterfall of numbers? Certainly. Here is your answer: to illustrate the bigness and goodness of our God. How big is that bigness? Isn't it enough to make our universe appear a walk in the park, considering our God's infinite and eternal omnipresence, omnipotence, and omniscience?

Okay, here is but a taste of His goodness: He created all things (Gen. 1:1) and holds them together (Col. 1:17), is not a God of confusion (1 Cor. 14:33) but can manage His creation even if His creatures cannot (Ps. 24:1). He knows the beginning from the end (Isa. 46:10), is everywhere (omnipresent, Jer. 23:23–24), knows everything (omniscient, Ps. 147:5), and is all-powerful (omnipotent, 2 Chron. 20:6).

And how good is His goodness? He is all about loving and caring for humans: He has numbered our days (Ps. 139:16), has a plan for our lives (Jer. 29:11), predestined us (Eph. 1:11–12), knit us together in our mothers' wombs (Ps. 139:13), has never left or forsaken us (Deut. 31:8), carved our names on the palms of His hands (Isa. 49:16), carries us (Ps. 28:8), knows our thoughts before we have them (Ps. 94:11), and knows all about our future (John 16:13).

I may have lost a portion of my readers to intractable religious

dogma, treasured traditional teachings, or ethnocentric denomina-
tional doctrines when asked to believe that the Lord took time to
audibly speak in that motel room on I-70, inaudibly on the way to
Concordia—and all to deliver a command to an errant Christian man
hours later in a gas station (for Heaven's sake) to keep the sin of fornica-
tion from infecting him and his budding relationship with a Christian
woman in another town. Then, are we to believe that God is equally
concerned (Acts 10:34) for the world's remaining two billion five hundred million Christians over whom He watches (2 Chron. 16:9) in the
same way to keep sin's stain from each heart as He did with Jesse's?

How is that possible? The preceding discussion about the bigness of our God should make nothing impossible for Him, even to
the doubting Thomases among us. That we cannot wrap our finite
minds around an infinite God and then question what He can or cannot do is unworthy of comment (Mark 9:23), if not beyond the pale.
Then the question arises, begging the goodness of God. Is keeping sin
from our lives important enough for God to guard every blood-borne
Christian day and night from its stain? That it took (and takes) the
sacrificial blood of His only Son Jesus (as an ongoing cleansing of our
consciences, transgressions, and temptations) to keep us in fellowship
with Himself should put that question to rest.

While ruminating through this narrative, readers may wonder:
Wasn't the Lord's interest in Jesse's journey atypical and easy to write
off as chance, a fluke, atypical, or an anomaly? Really? If our God
(and His Word) is who He says He is, does what He says He does, is no
respecter of persons, impartial, and His roaming eyes seek to order
every Christian's step during every second of every day (2 Chron.
16:9), what is our problem here? If our omnipresent, omnipotent,
and omniscient God can name and track 200 billion trillion stars
within His 96 billion light-years of universe while simultaneously
accounting for innumerable daily events on Earth, how difficult is it
for Him to hover over a couple billion of His children to whom He is

committed to keep from the jaws of sin and in fellowship with Him on this tiny blue sphere?

If we can believe, then it takes little for a God so big and good to care deeply for humans like Jesse—and for little people like the both of us, His beloveds (Col. 3:12), His special treasures (Deut.14:2). And for those to whom He has given His all (Jesus, our Messiah, and His only Son) to keep us all reconciled and in fellowship with Him, doesn't the ravishing others-centered love of God make Jesus, who has created all things and makes it all possible, our most treasured Kiss from Heaven ever?

QUESTION: Where is the Kiss from Heaven from this God Story?

ANSWER: How about the Lord God Almighty sending your heart into a full-fledged tachycardia with His finest command voice booming, "Go to Concordia!" in the dead still of a pitch-black Missouri motel room as a start? Here's a guarantee: Sometimes supernatural interventions feel less like Kisses from Heaven than my drill instructor dressing me down for "misplacing" (he eagerly insisted I use the word "lost") my "cover" (Marine lingo for "cap") to jumpstart another day through the Marine Corps Officer Training School at Quantico, Virginia, in 1963. (Ask Moses about similar quality responses he received from Heaven.)

Then, as we followed His instructions with a trip to Concordia, He added an authoritative message: "No, absolutely no" by an inner voice and an identical banner headline and outside phone booth by inner visions. Didn't the obedient completion of the journey—all the way through delivering the message to Jesse and his collapse into confession (admission of sin), repentance (changing his mind), and conversion (turning his behavior about)—amaze you? Doesn't this demonstration of the Lord's desire for intimacy, His wonderous character, benevolent intent, lesson teaching, and bringing glory due His name make this an unchallengeable God Story? Then, as a testimony to Jesus' extraordinary divine intervention (miracle) in Jesse's life, the whole scenario became a Kiss from Heaven, a testimony full of deliverance and inner healing (mind renewal) for Jesse, and glory to Father for saving the man from sin and renewing his walk with Heaven.

And for those of us who question our Lord's ability to simultaneously tend to the needs of two billion five hundred million Christians on Earth, comfort yourselves by knowing He is simultaneously tending a much busier job, the needs of over two billion trillion stars in the vast expanse of His heavens (of which we are but privy to only a fraction) at the same moment.

♥ 16

The Big Red Ditch (1998)

For a former military aviator to have an acrophobia (fear of heights) is unusual, a tad humiliating, and something his old squadron mates must never know. For yours truly, commanding the cockpit of a military jet aircraft exceeding the sound barrier in a vertical dive from forty-thousand feet had been an outstanding rush. However, put me atop the Empire State Building, Lady Liberty's torch, that lighthouse on Cape Hatteras, or overlooking the Grand Canyon, where we were reluctantly standing, and I would go directly from "rocket man" to "rubber man." Wobbling like an oversized Gumby on the way back to our RV park, a full football field from that big red ditch, I wondered if our visit to one of this world's natural wonders was worth spending the night in a snowdrift following a losing battle with a monster blizzard on Interstate 40 south of Flagstaff for twenty minutes worth of weak knees, queasy stomach, and lightheadedness. How I needed to deal with that phobia.

Overnighting in that RV park was like trying to catch restful sleep in the brass section of the New York Philharmonic. For eight hours, two mighty bull elk bugled on the park's opposing fringes, trying to coerce each other into handing over hard-earned territorial rights without a tussle. Trapped in the epicenter of their land dispute, we had little to do but spend the entire night smothering our ears beneath an inadequate score of pillows. The dawn's early light signaled "bedtime" for the elk, so at least someone would get a little sleep. Cleaning up, we left for church.

The gathering was small, six to be exact. It would have been seven, but the pastor's wife had a virus, a sick child, or simply needed a holiday from her husband's all too familiar but enjoyable euphemisms. No one made that clear. The worship leader was a slim Irish lass in her early twenties with long, curly red hair and a voice that "near missed" its enthusiastic way through three melodies and their lyrics. She was the entire supporting cast in this little body and jumpy as a cat on a hot tin roof about it. Brief and to the point, the pastor was way done with his message before the pot roast had a chance. So, on our way out the door, and as is His fashion, Holy Spirit asked that we take the young woman worship leader to lunch.

Lunch on Us

Well, that usually meant another divine intercept. The lass was initially reluctant, but after a minute or two of easy conversation, we followed her to a favorite restaurant hanging over the canyon's edge. During our brief introductions and small talk, we discovered that she was a native of Ireland working on a green card in this little settlement bordering the national park.

Raised in and out of Catholicism, she had not been a born-again Christian long but was now a proud member of the intimate little church we had attended. Abruptly, and without completing her current thought, she broke off the conversation, excused herself, and hastily left for the restroom. How she left us seemed odd. We became concerned when, after twenty minutes, she had not returned.

Had we offended her? Was she ill? Afraid? We could not fathom her puzzling behavior, which, happily, was short-lived. Arriving from the restroom, she apologized for her sudden departure and forthrightly shared a confession: She was in an off-and-on relationship with a non-Christian man over which Holy Spirit was relentlessly convicting her for being unequally yoked. Her anxiety was affecting her work and ministry. She did not know what to do, but she was certain we were the people to help her.

Now, as inner healing ministers, that always raises a red flag for us. Emotional pain seeks comfort in as easy a way out as possible. Humans often forage through forests of other humans' advice until they find what they want to hear while disregarding the wisdom from above they reject along the way. This felt like we were in that filter again until she continued.

"This is a small town, and, being relatively new here, I have no trustworthy friends. I do not feel I can share my dilemma with the pastor, and any other acquaintances might be unreliable. Last night, on my knees, I asked the Lord to bring me counsel from people who were total strangers both to me and this town. When Jesus called me to the restroom, He confirmed you were those people."

Well, at least we now understood her sudden, bizarre departure.

Holy Spirit had once again set the stage, so quickly assuming our roles, we buckled down to quality time in ministry. At its end, our now forgiven, enlightened, determined, and confident little sister left, transformed by the renewing of her mind by Holy Spirit (Rom. 12:2) and equipped with everything necessary to make and execute a godly decision to end her dilemma; we knew she would. Once again, Jesus had orchestrated a divine intercept and another Kiss from Heaven to help one of His children back to full-time fellowship with Him.

Peering from the restaurant's picture window into the vast cavernous expanse below, I could not tell whether my queasy stomach came from wolfing down that greasy hamburger at lunch or looking down the gullet of that big red ditch again. In either case, after ponying up enough cash from Emily's big black bag to pay for our table's lunch, this teetering little burg on the edge of that big red ditch was about to become but another blessed entry in dear Holy Spirit's wondrous journal.

Postscript

If we listen to and obey Him, the Lord is so good at setting up situations for ministry, isn't He? Here we were on our roundabout return to Oregon from Texas when an unseasonable snowstorm sidelined us for an overnight on Interstate 40 and again at the Grand Canyon, followed by early services at a little church the next morning. Unbeknown to us, a young woman in a messy situation had been crying desperately to the Lord for help—not just for help in a generic sense, mind you, but help from total strangers. So, camouflaged as an innocent invitation to lunch, Jesus orchestrated a divine appointment in a local restaurant between the young woman and those strangers she had requested—a pair of inner healing ministers tactically delayed and then diverted through her little town on the way to their home in Oregon. Then, to relieve her anxiety, He called the young woman to the restroom to confirm her lunchmates as the help for which she had prayed the previous evening. At long last, ministry underway and ministry complete.

On behalf of what number of hurting people worldwide is Holy Spirit asking believers with "ears to hear" at this moment to buy lunch as a first step toward another saint's divine healing? Millions would be my estimate, especially if it is Sunday (or Saturday with the Sabbath keepers).

Don't we all long to see the days of Heaven on Earth when multitudes of Christians routinely gather worldwide after church at their favorite restaurants to give and receive ministry? Of course. While we are at it, let us not forget to thank each one of this planet's gracious restaurateurs who make a living from those Christian-sponsored meals and, lest we seem ill-mannered, briefly spend some love on those gracious, others-centered inner healing ministers who don't. Is that a pea under our mattress, Princess Emily?

QUESTION: Where is the Kiss from Heaven from this God Story?

ANSWER: Is an answer to prayer a miracle? By all means. It is the very essence of a miracle as defined by the Merriam-Webster Dictionary. So when our hero in this God Story knelt by her bedside crying out for help from strangers (to both her and the town), it started in motion a Heaven-sent plan that had temporarily taken Emily and me out of commission by an unexpected blizzard as we approached the Grand Canyon two days before. Then, enter Holy Spirit, setting up a lunch meeting after church to satisfy our young friend's answer to her previous night's prayer for ministry from strangers by putting us back in commission. Kiss from Heaven received. Often, the Lord greases the skids and sets the stage well in advance, putting into motion a well-orchestrated and exquisitely timed event we commonly, but incorrectly, interpret as a spontaneous or coincidental one. Silly us, as unbelievers. Shame on us, if He is our ever-present Lord.

The Saga of Lonnie Noblet (2005)

Space heaters blasting hot air into the storage bays of our thirty-three-foot Monaco RV had barely kept the water pipes from freezing during our trip through northeast Arkansas's minus-seven-degree Fahrenheit cold spell. Now, here we were, two days later in Dallas, facing short-sleeve weather at Christmastime. Old Man Winter was becoming schizoid; what was this topsy-turvy climate change stuff, anyway? Emily, my Proverbs 31 wife, preoccupied by her grandma's gene, had quickly made a beeline to the local Walmart in a desperate search for stocking stuffers for the grandchildren while I rummaged through our summer clothing, now retired, and packed behind those heroic storage bay heaters to find something to wear more in keeping with the weather.

The store was teeming with patrons gathering last-minute items. With all the Walmart faithful bustling about her, Emily was having difficulty finding an associate free to help. At last, she cornered one bright-blue-vested employee, a janitor she later discovered, who happily led her in the right direction. Exchanging small talk on the way, Emily discovered that he had no local family and was to spend the upcoming holiday alone. Her heart went out to him, not an unusual response for my kind wife, and she felt it would please the Lord to find him a way to celebrate Christmas. Per her routine, she recruited her reliably reluctant husband as an accomplice.

Lonnie Noblet would not have been a noteworthy person had it not been for his full white "Santa-esque" beard, weathered red face, and broad-as-a-Texas-prairie paunch. Meeting Lonnie might have been like meeting Jolly Old Saint Nick himself, but for one small item: Lonnie Noblet was by no means a jolly old man but more a fuzzy peach topside and a prickly pear below decks. Still, Emily and I agreed a man in his midsixties, alone with little joy and no family at hand who enters your life at Christmastime, should qualify as a "divine intercept."

At first, we stunned our St. Nick look-alike, the object of wide-eyed awe from all his young passersby, with our Christmas Eve dinner invitation but soon convinced him to join us. Gathering gifts for our new-found friend, we left for home. The saga of Lonnie Noblet had begun.

Small Talk and Lots of It

We gathered Lonnie up the following evening, now crisper after another celebrated Dallas weather change. Settling on a little Thai restaurant, we hit our chairs, already engrossed in a one-way conversation. From the start, Lonnie was busy sharing stories about his childhood, work history, and, finally, his experiences in the military. Listening, his life gradually took on meaning like a puzzle, joined one painful storied piece to another, until the sum of his days rumbled forth as a lifetime filled with hardship. Among others, we could hear voices of emotionally wounded military warriors for whom we had cared over the years echoing from this solitary, disillusioned, angry, and lonely man. His was a voice furious with a government that he felt had used, betrayed, and discarded him. It was the easily recognizable voice of a Vietnam combat veteran.

Lonnie Noblet had become incensed, his words harsh and his tone of voice piercing. There he had been at 2:30 a.m. on a pitch-black, moonless, October night fifty miles west of his base in Chu Lai, Republic of Vietnam. Dropped by Huey choppers along with his entire company into a predetermined jungle landing zone (LZ), the object of that night's mission was to interrupt an enemy supply line tasked with supplying Viet Cong outposts with mortars and rockets meant to hinder flight operations from Chu Lai's airstrips.

Regrettably, the infantry company had met with heavy firepower from overwhelming numbers of North Vietnamese regulars who gradually forced Lonnie's outnumbered infantry into a tightening circle of defense. Dug in with mortars raining bedlam, our warrior had been too busy staying alive to be frightened but not too busy to feel deep rage at an "incompetent government" who had not only recklessly conscripted him into this war but more so had no intention of extricating him from tonight's firefight. Convinced this night would be his last, Lonnie was furious about it.

A Rude Awakening

At the exact terror-ridden moment over forty years before when Lonnie Noblet believed he was going to die in a firefight with the North Vietnamese, four Marine aviators were being scrambled from a deep sleep at 0240 hours. In the pitch-black of our hooch, one of many open-sided plywood shells where aviators slept and stored their gear, an unidentifiable Marine, his voice brimming with unmistakable urgency, was vigorously shaking us four pilots one after the other from our reveries. Because Chu Lai was on the shores of the South China Sea, soothing tropical sea breezes helped promote restful sleep after long days commonly filled with two to three combat flights and extensive collateral duties. (The squadron's busy S-1 administrative officer was my assignment.) Considering the urgency of the mission while shedding our sleep demons, we hastily threw on our layered gear and raced through the sand toward the flight line where four aircraft, "loaded for bear," stood ready.

The VMA 223 Bulldogs, a fixed-wing Marine attack squadron, flew the A4E Skyhawk, a single-seat low-level ground support jet aircraft with a maximum takeoff weight of 24,500 pounds, where over 8,600 of those pounds were ordinance. The aircraft, dubbed "Scooter" by its beloved aviators, was the sports car of jet attack aircraft and, as Mohammed Ali in his prime claimed, could "float like a butterfly but sting like a bee." Diminutive as it was (only three feet longer but two tons lighter than my elderly Country Coach RV), it was nimble and quick, always the welcome hero among our ground troops but a legendary anathema reviled by the enemy.

One of the aircraft's primary missions was to soften up targets on the ground, letting Marines move forward toward their objectives. It was dangerous work if only because the enemy was becoming proficient using fifty-caliber ground fire against aircraft while the new SAM III ground-to-air missiles, recently introduced into the "demilitarized zone" (DMZ) to the north, were another force to be reckoned with. We were uncertain what was going down that night, but by the sound of things, we could expect a challenge.

Over the ponderous sand dune to the west of our sleeping quarters, its summit occupied by the squadron's command post (CP), was the SATS (short airfield for tactical support) runway. Executing a takeoff on that runway was always a carnival ride of sorts, as it was constructed from AM-2 aluminum alloy planks (twelve feet long by two feet wide by two inches thick, and each weighing 144 pounds) joined and resting on 8,000 feet of reinforced sand (leave it to a Marine to reinforce sand; actually, we can thank the Navy Seabees who spent years solving that problem). On takeoff, the aircraft would sway this way and that over the unstable terrain and struggle to separate itself from earth under its heavy load of ordinance. Only dimly flickering and unreliable, ancient kerosene construction flare pots lined each side of the strip, leaving the plane's taxi light in charge of keeping the aircraft's takeoff and landing paths visible in the darkness.

Early that morning, our "birds" bristled with racks of 500-pound bombs. Our division leader (a division is a flight of two sections with two planes per section) radioed there was an infantry company (varying between 50 and 200 men) pinned down in a raging firefight against overpowering numbers of North Vietnamese regulars fifty miles to the west. Our ground pounders desperately needed an immediate escape route. West, the mountains were shrouded in darkness, and close air support in the mountains in the dead of night was always a test and often a crapshoot. Add a trapped unit of fighting men struggling to extricate themselves from overwhelming odds to the mix, and we had our hands full. Those men on the ground? Simple. There were too few, no more on the way, and it was up to us. That was too much to dwell on.

After shaking and baking our way one after the other down that wavy ribbon of runway to become airborne, we joined up, headed west in formation, and within minutes approached the target area.

A Desperate Situation

The forward air controller (FAC), a war-hardened, experienced aviator stationed with those beleaguered warriors somewhere in the inky blackness below, was busy over the airwaves; the situation on the ground had deteriorated and threatened to become untenable as the massive enemy force steadily closed on the embattled Americans. The FAC's responsibility would be to direct the air strike, a task fraught with potential pitfalls, including everything from missing the unseen target altogether to incurring collateral friendly fire casualties among our troops. For the aviators, it could mean losing an aircraft to a mountainside or enemy fifty caliber or small arms fire. The FAC's calculations would decide both the fate of his company and our aircraft. If those calculations were exact and we failed to observe them, the outcome could be tragic. Precise teamwork would be essential. He relayed that his men were experiencing increasingly heavy fire and could momentarily expect the North Vietnamese to overrun their company's defenses. It was imperative for the aviators, he emphasized, to drop their ordinance ASAP and precisely according to his instructions. There were but feet of separation from the enemy, he hollered above the din of battle. The chaos below was palpable over the airways, and in the cockpit, perspiration trickled down the back of my neck.

The FAC went on; he would fire a white phosphorous flare several thousand feet aloft to drift slowly through the still night air suspended by a mini parachute. Although this would create a surreal and disorienting light in the inky darkness, magnified by eerie shadows cast upon the black terrain below, it would give the aviators an essential reference point to establish a correct heading for our bombing runs. The FAC would broadcast that heading, followed by the airspeed, dive angle, and altitude to release bombs and initiate pullouts.

Two things were abundantly clear: The FAC had a life-threatening dilemma, and his instructions were inalterable. As exacting as those instructions had to be to ensure his escape, they had to be unerring for the precise delivery of our ordinance. There was no wiggle room for error. We also knew these uncertain conditions might demand more than we or our aircraft could accurately deliver. This was no practice run, and if there were fifty-caliber fire from below, it would be deadly. In true Marine grit, our flight leader had but one stiff reply to the FAC: "Wilco (will comply)."

In the Guts of the Mission

Within seconds, our flight leader broadcast the commencement of his run, "Number one, rolling in." Lights out to reduce the chances of being an easier target, the ink swallowed up his aircraft. Circling above, we waited. A terse "number one, off target" announced the completion of his run. Like clockwork, his wingman radioed, "Number two, rolling in," followed shortly by his "number two, off target." That was my signal; lights out, I transmitted, "Number three, rolling in," while simultaneously pushing the Skyhawk's nose over into the lighted black hole below.

The aircraft's instrument lights cast a soft red glow about the cockpit while the radio rested in silence. But for the regular, if slightly quickened, breathing issuing from my oxygen mask, the surroundings were silent. Carefully setting up the assigned dive angle and airspeed of 250 knots on the FAC's heading, I scanned my instrument panel for confirmation of my position in space. Like any aviator with over one thousand hours in a single model aircraft, I had long ago become "fused" with this bird, a oneness that kept me ahead of the aircraft, staying beyond the moment to anticipate what would or could follow. Moving to align our descent with the flare, I avoided direct eye contact so as not to lose night vision or precipitate disabling vertigo, a lesson aviators often learn the hard way. Passing the burning phosphorous, the aircraft and I fine-tuned our required instrument parameters as we entered that eerie paradox of lighted blackness.

Adding to the subtle tension (a eustress condition normally experienced by humans during intense times to help hone our attention and place our bodies and minds on high alert), there was even more urgency to meet the stringent parameters issued by the FAC. We knew this would be a life-and-death defining mission for all concerned. Still, unlike those troops on the ground, the aviators would face only unseen and unheard enemy fire (unless hit), which helped concentrate on precision delivery of the ordinance. However, there lurked one delicate yet unspoken "elephant in the living room" at these times: Could we depend upon the judgment and essential skills of the FAC locked in his desperate life-and-death struggle mere hundreds of feet below?

Under the current stress, would he take needless chances with our lives to save the men about him and himself to thread the eye of tonight's needle? Never. Was he trusting us to stretch our aircrafts' envelopes and our abilities to thread that needle? There was no doubt about that. The FAC and the remaining warriors with him were but mere feet away from the enemy and severely at risk of becoming collateral damage due to our friendly fire. Trust in the success of our mission was all they had left.

The FAC did not need to remind us to maintain a wings-level attitude on pullout before entering a tight four-G, 180 degrees of turn and climb after delivering our ordinance. Not doing so could cause a sudden snap roll (due to asymmetric wing lift), a quirk peculiar to the Skyhawk and other aircraft in the past, followed by an uncontrolled impact with the ground. Complicating matters in the inky blackness would be an unseen dead-end valley ahead and the proximity of an immovable mountain to starboard, both demanding an immediate exit. Running into either would be an unforgiving experience. Moment by moment, any latitude in this mission became more of a pipedream.

Eyes glued to my cockpit's instrument panel while watching the altimeter rapidly unwind to the designated release altitude, I pickled (dropped) the ordinance. In true Skyhawk fashion, the nose of the now-lightened bird automatically pitched upward, helping me apply steady back pressure to the stick to raise the nose wings-level above my gyroscope's artificial horizon. Calling, "Off target," jamming full power, snapping the aircraft into a ninety-degree right bank, and pulling through the four-G turn required was a simultaneous coordinated move.

Truth told, the turn exceeded five Gs and into a tad of buffet (stall warning). This maneuver instantly filled my G-suit's belly, thigh, and calf bladders with air pressure, reduced blood flow into both legs, and continued to perfuse my brain with oxygen-rich blood, leaving enough central vision to read the instruments.

Knowing there was a mountain waiting out there, the reality of being in the hands of a veteran FAC and my own years of fleet experience gratefully came rushing home. So far, so good. Completing the turn through 180 degrees, the intrepid little aircraft continued her now-established ascent to altitude. Marine teamwork had triumphed again? I did not yet know the half of it. Number four was calling, "Off target."

All Is Well That Ends Well

It was not long before we had a company of jubilant fighting men celebrating as background noise during the FAC's deliriously unprofessional radio transmissions. It was such a rewarding feeling to hear the joy mixed with relief in his voice. A sprinkling of those bombs had landed too close for comfort, but there was not a scratch among our troops. That was not true for the enemy. The air strike had obliterated his perimeter and routed his regulars. All resistance had stopped, and the beleaguered Americans, now liberated, had regrouped and were swiftly returning to their LZ—a successful evacuation with no man left behind.

What Were the Chances

As Lonnie relived that ancient battle at our Christmas Eve supper, his words across the table were becoming tense and emphatic. Besieged and nearly overrun, the company commander had launched a phosphorous flare aloft, which bathed the entire area in pale green fluorescence. Hoping beyond hope that help was imminent, the entire company had, in unison, recognized the distinct sounds of Skyhawk turbines overhead. Within seconds, bombs impacted in such proximity that the ground shook while shrapnel pierced the foliage directly above Lonnie's head as he glued himself to the ground. Time after time, the ordinance struck the center of its target, shaking the earth and pounding the enemy positions to force the North Vietnamese troops to flee in chaos and panic. Within seconds of the air strike, the jungle, except for the occasional distressed calls from North Vietnamese wounded, was again silent. Then it erupted in celebration.

Lonnie had to pinch himself to see if he was alive. Man, oh man, he loved those A4 Skyhawk drivers.

Eyes riveted on our evening's guest while processing what he had so emotionally shared, I blurted out, "Lonnie, one of those birds was mine." The old duffer, now speechless for the first time that evening, could only stare at me. We double checked the dates. We double checked the location. We double checked the time. We double checked the circumstances. There was no doubt about it. How dumbfounded were we, three mannequins glued to our chairs around that table. Approaching four decades later and one-half a world away, what was the chance that two comrades in arms would meet again in such an unusual way? After mission upon mission in Vietnam and all those intervening years, I had at last met, face-to-face, a fighting man whose safety I helped secure while Lonnie finally found closure to the most horrific night of his life.

Looking across the table at this messed up, old-before-his-time, distraught Vietnam veteran struggling to gain a foothold in his current struggle with life, had anything of substance changed for him? And what favor had our four-plane mission done that night? Had he not simply exchanged one dire battle in his forlorn life for another? So here was Lonnie Noblet, now part of my history, the day before celebrating our Savior's birth, a broken man, virtually friendless and with no visible family. How does one respond to a Christian brother at such a time? Sweet Emily and I shared the same thought.

A Perfect Conclusion

Leaving that Thai restaurant, we drove to my son's home, where our extended family had gathered to celebrate a Merry Christmas Eve. People packed the place, and I wondered if the folks were not a tad uncomfortable having this salty relic of days gone by lounging about their upscale living room brimming with successful men, fashionable women, and privileged children. If so, that concern quickly vanished when my two-year-old granddaughter, Addison, wide-eyed and beaming, arrived on the scene and boldly approached Lonnie. Waggling her tiny index finger at this familiar-looking stranger, who was no stranger at all, she squealed with delight, "Ho, Ho," and again and again, "Ho, Ho, Ho."

"Well, Addie," I mused quietly, "aren't we in complete agreement? After the gift this brother and I exchanged tonight, it appears as if Santa has come a bit early this year for all of us." Glancing at Lonnie engulfed by one giant smile was enough. "Kiss from Heaven received, Lord, and, by the way, Jesus, an incredibly Happy Birthday."

Then, I reminded myself to thank Emily for, well, for being Emily and obeying Jesus one more time—again.

Postscript

Wasn't this meeting an improbable defying of the odds thirty-eight years beyond and a half a world away from Lonnie's and my shared battleground experience? As Christians, we should always view such meetings as carefully planned intercepts by God (Ps. 37:23) rather than random events. "Impossible," unbelievers would say, to which we as Christians must respond, "Not to a God who has named and maintains two hundred billion trillion stars rocketing through our universe at one hundred forty-five million miles per hour while on an average day simultaneously ordering seventeen trillion two hundred billion steps of two billion five hundred million Christians on this tiny blue globe."

In retrospect and considering the above, our meeting with Lonnie Noblet, which admittedly had a lengthy list of moving parts, surely took but minutes and few design skills of an apprentice junior-grade angel to engineer. But why the intercept in the first place? Well, didn't Jesus know, above all things, that Lonnie needed a barrel full of reinforced unconditional love after having lived such a seemingly barren and unproductive life? But why love? Because love never fails (1 Cor.

13:8). Then, why us? Don't you think Father wanted Lonnie to know that the same Lord who loved and rescued him in Chu Lai years before was giving notice that He had not forgotten the man and still had a plan for his life? Oh, had we known!

That Jesus is the alpha, the beginning of all good things in our lives, is something of which we are aware while forgetting that He is also the omega, the ending of all good things in our lives. What Jesus starts, He finishes. And finishing the job well is one of His hallmarks (John 19:30). And remember: All things work together for good for those who love God and are called according to His purposes (Rom. 8:28). If those thoughts elevate your curiosity, keep blazing the trail we are on, Christian. Then, watch our loving God at His absolute best.

QUESTION: Where is the Kiss from Heaven found in this God Story?

ANSWER: "Love never fails" (1 Cor. 13:8). So, let's be clear: This incredible God Story would have never surfaced had my dear and kindest wife, Emily, not decided Lonnie Noblet, an old, blue-vested Walmart janitor, porcupine, and Santa wannabe, needed a little TLC, a few gifts, and a good meal to rescue him from a lonely Christmas Eve. Then, as our evening's centerpiece, we discovered how our Marine flight of A-4 Skyhawks made Lonnie and his company a way where there was no way; it was breathtaking for all of us. But what you have yet to discover is that saving Lonnie's life led to something glorious enough to make this story a mere segue for the next. Keep reading, Christian, and see why with God (move over Yogi Berra), "It's not over 'til it's over."

18

The Saga of Lonnie Noblet Continues, As Sagas Do (2007–2017)

Christmases later, we found Lonnie Noblet living in a Fort Worth mission during our visit. He had not changed except for having become more of a porcupine. It is always hard for an angry man like Lonnie to bow to all the rigid rules and regulations required by any homeless shelter. His life seemed a slippery slope, so common for an aging Vietnam veteran who once proudly and independently cared for himself and others but was now forced to depend on impersonal systems he long ago came to despise.

We took Lonnie to dinner at my daughter-in-law's parents' place, spent the evening chatting with him and people we hardly knew, and then returned our friend, gifts in hand, to his mission "home." Void of the exciting rhetoric and comradery that had punctuated the wartime bonding experience during our first visit, this episode with Lonnie seemed somehow hollow and disconnected. We did not intend for the evening to end on such an emotionally discordant note. We had hoped for more. Regrettably, Lonnie's life seemed to have changed for the worse, not the better, as we again parted ways.

Then, two years later, we Googled Lonnie's whereabouts on a

Thanksgiving Day. He was living in still another inner-city mission. With our grandkids in tow, along with a whole slew of gifts, gobblers, and honeyed hams, we headed to Fort Worth. Privacy laws as they are, the mission could no longer reveal whether Lonnie was a resident, was not open to message him, nor let us search the premises for our man's whereabouts. Sadly, we left thankless on what, otherwise, was a lovely Thanksgiving Day.

A Half-Dozen Years Later

Six years later, Emily and I found ourselves again in Fort Worth for a short sojourn, which turned into two months of convincing our RV to cowboy up following maladies caused by too many years of deconditioning and disuse. While waiting for the old guy to complete rehab (that would be the RV, not me—although I was without doubt in the running), one day, Emily had a thought: "Let's see if we can locate Lonnie." Sounded good, although a little iffy. Ten years was a sizable interval; the man was already looking a little like Methuselah at our last get-together.

As a wise husband, I chose not to point out the obvious, which would have been, "Hey, Emily, if we could not contact him as a sick, down-and-out mission-dweller six years ago, what are the odds of finding him today?" Minutes later, Emily reappeared with the address of the only Lonnie Noblet, it appeared, on the entire planet. And "eureka," he lived but twelve minutes away by car and less than six, Emily continued by rubbing in the salt, as the crow flies. Was that the same crow I came near to eating for that evening's meal? May I reemphasize the "wise husband" quote to save a little face?

That afternoon, we piled into Little Red, our 2001 Chevy Tracker tow car, stoked up the Garmin GPS, and followed that little fella's pointy lavender finger all the way to Lonnie's address. "Bummer," I thought, as we did everything from threatening to knock down the door, nearly breaking a window, and finally, in desperation, hollering straight up the dryer vent to roust Lonnie from his modest abode. We were about to enter our second Lonnie Noblet funk in the same number of visits when who drives up in a fancy ride but the man himself. For a second, he looked unsettled as we raced, hollering our names across his front lawn.

A Last Supper

Then, the old guy lit up like Mrs. O'Leary's cowshed. "Oh!" he cried. "I have been thinking about you two every day for years." Within minutes, we had a big-time dinner date planned for Friday night in a local steakhouse. That visit began strikingly like the first celebration we shared years before. But this time, as the man once again carried the conversation, his mood was not one of dissatisfaction and anger but of overwhelming gratitude and joy.

What, I thought, *has happened to this guy? He is praising Jesus every other word for his blessed life.* That we found his major personality change puzzling is an understatement. While I pondered this perplexing scenario, Lonnie suddenly digressed to Vietnam.

Well, okay, here it comes, I thought while preparing for the predictable salvos of hate and discontent.

But instead of cursing the government and the military, Lonnie centered on countless children with cleft palates and hair lips (long associated with but lacking proven causation by the defoliant Agent Orange and other dioxin-contaminated herbicides used by the United States in Vietnam) that he had met "in country" in the 1960s. "Time after time," he continued, "I promised the Lord that I would take care of those kids if He would supply me with the funds when I returned to the States."

Well, my thought—not a real shocker—was snarky and devoid of any faith: "Lord, how did that work out for you?" Now, pay attention, Christian; Lonnie is about to have a God-breathed answer to that faithless question for the both of us.

"Decades later," our friend continued, "I filed for a VA (Department of Veterans Affairs) disability. Nothing happened, so I concluded nothing would. Then, after seven years, I received a letter from the Veterans Administration awarding me a 100 percent disability, which meant $3,000 per month for life with an added accumulated one-time award based on the time since my filing of $245,000. I quickly invested that money in the market. It did well."

Struggling to stay afloat with these words, Emily and I nearly needed life support as he continued: "So I have been able, on the average, to pay for one child's cleft palate surgical repair per month. This month, I will do three. The Lord heard my cry from Vietnam and has answered my prayers. Now, I can help those kids, just as I promised, because Jesus gave me the funds." (Then Lonnie quietly mentioned that he had given over $100,000 to this cause over the last four years.) "I live to give," Lonnie smiled, "and give to live."

It is hard to put into words the gears Emily and I had to shift through to catch up to that moment. It seemed but yesterday we sat across a table from someone who looked identical to the someone sitting there that evening. But this was a different someone, a truly others-centered, reformed curmudgeon. The overt anger, rage, and bitterness were gone. Instead, here sat a grateful, buoyant man, full of joy, eyes welling over with tears at every turn and full of the love of Jesus.

Emily and I stared at each other in amazement, but why? The Lord had merely been true to His Word again: "But just as it is written, things which eye has not seen and ear has not heard, and which have not entered the heart of man, all that God has prepared for those who love Him" (1 Cor. 2:9).

Postscript

Life brings us opportunities like Lonnie, doesn't it? Defending Florence, the poorest little girl in our second-grade class, from a couple of bullies one day in a school stairwell, God smiled. As usual, her school outfit was a stained, raggedy dress; she needed a bath, stunk like a goat, and had a chronic sinus infection that constantly poured thick yellow discharge from both her nostrils. She was to teachers and students the only true "untouchable" in the entire school.

Honestly, as a kid, it was hard not to fall headlong into the student body's jokes and to shun her like the rest. What let me resist were the shoes Jesus had given me to walk in through my own childhood troubles, which, believe me, fell far short of Florence's in both quality and quantity. Still, in an important way, those shoes enabled me to slip with empathy into hers and, years later, thanks to Emily, into Lonnie's.

Isn't our world full of stinky, wounded "children" of all ages, draining the pus of rage, fear, rejection, shame, and countless other painful emotions birthed somewhere in a history of real trauma? These tortured folks, the "Lonnie Noblets" of this world, who first experience and then spew dysfunction over an entire lifetime, desperately need others to stand alongside them. Yet only the Lord knows the beginning from the end for every life He has created. Only He knows what lurks in the hearts of men. Only Jesus knew that Lonnie Noblet, a man of sorrows acquainted with grief himself, was trustworthy. Only Jesus knew that Lonnie was a man of his word and that the crucible that had been Lonnie's life was about to bring forth pure gold.

In Vietnam, Lonnie had invested his yet-inherited earthly riches by faith in a solemn promise to the Lord that remained cocooned for decades until, like the most beautiful of butterflies, one day took flight no longer as a dream but as a Heaven-sent reality, an unending parade of joyous children in a distant land beaming with newborn smiles. Heartwarming, is it not? But not really a surprise. Jesus told us that wherever we put our treasure (riches), there our hearts (desires) would be also (Matt. 6:21).

Wasn't Lonnie following Heaven's principle that the Lord had tried to impart to the rich young ruler (Matt. 19:21)? Pay it forward.

Every good gift comes from above (James 1:17). Give the gift away, and it will be given you, pressed down, shaken together, running over in multiplied measure (Luke 6:38). For Lonnie, paying forward the gift the Lord had given him (fulfilling his promise to Jesus by investing in the healing of countless cruelly deformed Vietnamese children) saw his gift pressed down, shaken together, and running over as a most endearing and enduring Kiss from Heaven, the presence and joy of the Lord (Ps. 16:11) that our hero had sought without satisfaction his entire life.

So the unending but ever-changing saga of Lonnie Noblet traveled on Kiss from Heaven to Kiss from Heaven until Lonnie, on his omega journey of joy, joined Jesus in 2017 to receive his next Kiss from Heaven in person.

See you in a bit, old friend.

QUESTION: Where is the Kiss from Heaven from this God Story?

ANSWER: Who says money cannot buy happiness? Nobody, when you do not love mammon more than Jesus. Wasn't Lonnie the poster boy for that statement? Integrity is simple, isn't it? Make your word your bond. Lonnie did. Then, look what came to pass. When we keep our promises, won't Jesus keep His? What promise have you made to our God of the impossible that He might bring you a Kiss from Heaven and testimony to His glory? It is never too late.

Funky Day Mission at
The Mission (2009)

Admittedly, I was in a spiritual funk and had been for weeks. Ever been in that place where Jesus is light-years away, and each prayer ricochets off your ceiling like a silver bullet from the Lone Ranger's six-shooter? How about when feeding on the Word tastes like day-old cardboard, when your heart is as tender as a Kevlar vest, or when you have all the mercy of a starved wolverine? Would someone please tell me why Jesus saunters into the room at those times with an assignment fit only for Mother Theresa? Am I the only one in this conversation?

Now we can expect beehives of earnest questions by religious folks that arise in such times like this: Was I snared secretly in sin, was I refusing to forgive, had I unresolved bitterness, was I living in betrayal, or ad infinitum? Could we consider this point: A large contingent of folks in the Bible had funky seasons too. How about Apostle Paul, "Wretched man that I am! Who will set me free from the body of this death?" (Rom. 7:24) or Prophet Elijah, "And I alone am left; and they seek my life, to take it away" (1 Kings 19:14) or King David, "Rescue me, O Lord, from evil men; Preserve me from violent men, Who devise evil things in *their* hearts" (Ps. 140:1–2) or Jeremiah (Jer. 38:6) in the muddy cistern or Jonah (Jon. 4:8) out from under the castor oil plant or Peter (Matt. 26:75) listening to that rooster crow for the third time?

Get the drift? God's people are real people who get into real funks for real reasons. His solutions for those times are purposeful, never wasted, and often to . . . well, let us look.

At the End of a Long Spiritual Rope

One morning, while dangling in prayer at the end of my spiritual rope, I heard Holy Spirit say, "Pray in the Spirit." It quickly dawned on me that His Word said, "For if I pray in a tongue, my spirit prays, but my mind is unfruitful" (I Cor. 14:14). He did not ask me to pray as I had with my mind to be fruitful but, rather, to "pray in the Spirit." Then, Holy Spirit took me to the scripture, "And in the same way the Spirit also helps our weakness; for we do not know how to pray (with our minds) as we should, but the Spirit Himself intercedes for us with groanings too deep for words" (Rom. 8:26, parenthetical mine). Evidently, Father's lack of response and my lack of fruit over the last weeks meant that in my present weakness, I had no idea of how to pray as I should to get out of this funk.

Aware that He did know how to pray and had said so, I obeyed Holy Spirit to the letter. He had said, "Pray in the Spirit," and in the Spirit would be how I sent my prayers until further notice. And sent they were, unfruitful to my mind as they were, an hour or so every morning, day after day. In a tug of war with Heaven, I had no idea what this contest was about nor who was winning. Yet I pressed on, undeterred by the incessant lies of Satan's harassing minions (you know that drill), my own impatience, and times of discouragement when I wished to abandon what seemed a sinking ship.

Early one dark, drizzly Oregon spring morning (as if there is any other in the Beaver State that time of year), while I was trying to find a fault line, any small fissure, or unlocked skylight to Heaven in that brass ceiling over my bed, Jesus finally spoke up: "I want you to go to the mission."

"Which one? The mission in Maui, Lord?" I might have pleaded had my feeble, sleep-infested brain been prepared for this intrusion.

"Eugene," injected Jesus, reading my unthought-of-thought. Well, so much for balmy spring mornings caressed by scented fragrances carried by gentle breezes over glassy seas and under crystal skies. But, hey, who was I to complain at this summons from above? At least my prayers were making it to the throne room.

Rolling my corpulent body from beneath the feathers, I looked aloft one more time at all that brass with renewed hope; for the first time in weeks, I knew with absolute certainty there must be a hairline fracture up there somewhere.

Now, Emily and our good friend Susan had a Bible study that morning, which left me, as the second member of a one-car family, with no transportation and facing a fifty-mile walk, were I to complete today's sudden assignment. Unknown to yours truly, the ladies' leader had canceled their weekly study, and the girls were heading for what else but a shopping spree in where else but Eugene, Oregon. Made aware, I asked them to drop me off at Railroad Street, but 200 yards from my destination.

Just a Closer Walk with Thee

When deposited alongside the tracks, I was awake enough to crave coffee and curious enough to wonder what Holy Spirit and I would do today. Certain that Jesus had a plan and desperate as I was for a God encounter, I mindlessly plunged into what threatened to become monsoon conditions in a part of town already drowning in a flood of despair.

Pausing briefly to buy java at a Korean-run mom-and-pop store, I struck up a conversation with the disinterested owner, who promptly struck it down for a television game show rerun on an elderly Zenith overhead his cash register.

Feeling a tad underappreciated, I scurried from the store, intentionally giving wide berth to a circle of rundown folks gathered into a tight circle, eagerly exchanging drugs for money. Doing that activity near the mission, they knew, would find them evicted in a heartbeat: you could not stop moving for a moment near that refuge without getting into hot water. In this part of town, the rules were different.

Walking with Jesus on the sidewalk within 100 feet of the main entrance to the mission complex and fast approaching the women's and children's shelter, a towering middle-aged man to my right was slowly overtaking me in the street. Looking every bit like a modern-day Paul Bunyan bundled in a black-and-red-checkered flannel shirt, sporting the broad suspenders and rugged jeans of a professional logger, he was losing all but a couple of rebellious wisps of hair to pattern baldness. Then I noticed the easily identifiable flushed face of a man smitten with a love for alcohol. Our eyes met at the precise time words poured forth from both our mouths. Slowing the pace, I gave way to his deep Southern drawl, unabashedly confessing a need to drink "a couple beers" before starting his morning hike into town as the way to overcome his dread of crowds.

Agoraphobia, an irrational fear of crowded places, leaving one's home, or being stuck where escape feels daunting, was my immediate diagnosis. Doctors label things if you haven't noticed.

While I was trying to swallow this tidbit, he was shifting gears into a detailed description of his neighbor's son sexually abusing him as a seven-year-old. Admittedly taken aback, I was trying to simultaneously choke down this added piece of news when he came to a screeching halt (against the rules at the mission, I might add) and raised his voice to a near shout: "Why am I telling you these things?" Without missing a beat, he looked up, pointed aloft, and continued, "Because He wants me to!"

Muted by my own astonishment offered Holy Spirit a chance to get a word in edgewise. He did: "Son, 'Paul' is today's assignment" (or something along these lines). Anyway, I got the message.

Real Street Ministry

Doing an about-face while initiating our brand of inner healing ministry with Paul (gratefully purloined from many who had gone before us), we picked up speed as I boldly asked my newest charge to relive that abuse memory in his mind, feel the emotion, and learn what he believed as a seven-year-old boy in that time of trauma. Without hesitation, he found, then entered that childhood memory and instantly experienced overwhelming feelings from that horror. When I asked what the little boy felt and believed, he replied, "I feel afraid (his painful feelings), as if I am trapped and going to die" (the belief that the little boy saw as truth and produced his fear). By design, and with Holy Spirit's help, we released anger toward the perpetrator in the memory—to ensure Holy Spirit's willingness to take an active part in the ministry by Paul repenting of his unforgiveness (Matt. 6:14–15)—then toward Paul himself for not resisting the abuse, and, finally, Father God for not coming to a swift rescue.

Once all offense, judgment, anger, and resulting unforgiveness (each a sin separating him from fellowship with the Spirit) were cleansed from the memory, Holy Spirit could bring truth to the little boy in Paul whose entire lifetime had been tortured by one lie believed as truth from one painful memory: "I am trapped and going to die." Can you see how that lie eventually gave rise to a lifetime of agoraphobia as an adult?

How did Jesus free little Paul from his inner pain even as he was reexperiencing the vivid memory of his abuse? By one truth, already logically but ineffectively known by Paul as an adult but requiring an experiential impartation of truth through an encounter with Holy Spirit by Paul's child: "You are not trapped, and you are not going to die." Easy, huh? Bringing the past up to date is not always so easy but here was simple. Adult logic cannot free us from painful lies believed as truth arising from traumatic childhood experience. Only an experiential encounter with Holy Spirit as our truth giver can impart the truth to set us free (John 8:32). Logic changes logic. Experience changes experience.

Significant traumatic experiences as adults with no history of similar childhood trauma can also produce their own lie-based pain by overwhelming events such as the horrors of war, rape, terror threats, or things unbearable like banishment from a family. Here, as in childhood trauma, logic will not be enough to replace experiential lies and their associated pain. Again, an experience demands a counter-experience—and that by an encounter with our Spirit of Truth.

Receiving the truth from Holy Spirit, Paul's child could now reenter a peaceful and calm but visually unaltered abuse memory. That he felt trapped and going to die now felt absurd and, try as he would, Paul could no longer experience the fear of death (emotional fear arising from the lie that he would die) from his entrapment during the abuse; in addition, he now felt compassion (rather than anger) and an even greater sense of forgiveness for his perpetrator as a part of the memory.

When Paul entered more recent memories as an adult, where he had routinely endured fear-ridden panic attacks and feelings of entrapment as manifestations of his agoraphobia, those emotions were now absent and, instead, a sense of peace and calm flooded those memories. In bringing the truth, "You are not trapped or going to die" (which dispelled the lie generated by his childhood trauma, "You are trapped and going to die"), it was now clear that the Lord had also dismantled Paul's agoraphobia triggered for years by fear of being trapped or having a limited ability to escape a sense of being trapped in densely populated places. Kiss from Heaven received. Thank you, Jesus.

An Encore

Within minutes, this intermittent mission-dweller recognized what his life-changing miracle meeting with Holy Spirit had meant. It took even less time for his floodgates to open again: His father had sold him to another man at age eleven.

Stepping back in disbelief, I stammered, "What? He sold you?"

Paul, nodding in affirmation, was an enormous contrast to the little eleven-year-old boy who suddenly appeared before my eyes, struggling to keep himself together.

"Let the emotion you are now feeling carry you to that time," I unintentionally barked while trying to seize the moment already happening.

Right away, little Paul was reexperiencing the "sale" memory, feeling his worthlessness, and knowing without a doubt he did not matter to his father. It was not long before Holy Spirit had helped us process his offense, judgment, anger, and unforgiveness toward his father, and little Paul was once again receiving the truth from Jesus to set him free. In an inner vision, as his perpetrator callously took him away, the Lord was holding his hand while saying, "You will always matter to Me." The sale memory, once so painfully traumatic that Paul kept it intentionally suppressed from his conscious mind, was suddenly calm, the lie, "I do not matter," no longer felt true, and the feeling of worthlessness had dissipated. At once, he entered a previously unknown sense of worth and value and knew in the depths of his heart, for the first time since his childhood, that he not only mattered to his earthly father, but he mattered more so to Jesus. Finally, while tears were flowing from Paul's eyes, compassion and forgiveness were flowing from his heart toward his troubled dad. "You shall know the truth and the truth shall make you free" (John 8:32). Second of today's Kisses from Heaven received, Lord. Thank you so much.

Singing in the Rain

Shortly after reaching the mission earlier that day and as forewarned, the weather severely deteriorated. Our first ministry session was not yet complete when the heavens opened, and a downpour flooded the pavement. Having no protective gear, this monsoon-like rain (a true metaphor for Holy Spirit Himself that day) quickly soaked us to our skins. Undaunted, we continued to press on like a couple of drenched river rats sloshing back and forth in front of the mission while oblivious to anything but hearing from Jesus for over ninety minutes. When Holy Spirit finished raining His truth on Paul, he and I exchanged a holy hug and parted. Paul found rapid refuge in the arms of the shelter just steps away; I had but exited the property when that ninety-minute downpour went to drizzling like a plugged spigot from Grandma's sink.

How heavy had been that rain? It took my leather shoes over a week to dry.

Postscript

"Is anyone among you sick? Let him call for the elders of the church, and let them pray over him, anointing him with oil in the name of the Lord; and the prayer offered in faith will restore the one who is sick, and the Lord will raise him up, and if he has committed sins, they will be forgiven him" (James 5:14–15). Have you ever considered why Jesus has asked us to leave our comfortable surroundings and tend to the prayer needs of the afflicted and needy? You might ask, "Why isn't it enough for a Christian who has a personal relationship with Christ to pray for his own needs?"

I will emphasize but one obvious reason here: Have you ever been sick unto death like Hezekiah (2 Kings 20:1), facing the wall and seeking to pray for yourself? Was it easy? Not by a long shot. However, Hezekiah did a laudable job while countless others (but not all) approaching Jesus for a healing touch without someone to "introduce" them (consider the paralytic requiring four friends to lower him through a roof to reach the Master) had failed on their own, hadn't they? Praying for our own needs is often overwhelming when hope is ebbing away, professional care has not altered the course of an illness, and a drug-induced coma or death seems the only workable alternative to suffering. Then, there is that infernal brass ceiling for those dealing with emotional and spiritual issues. In such times, Jesus calls upon His "elders" to be His heart and hands extended. In Hezekiah's case, let us remember Isaiah, the prophet, was nearby. And, praise Jesus, on that stormy day at the mission, for Paul, yours truly was so privileged.

Trapped by a major funk and into prayer in the Spirit to escape it, the Lord had on the sly recruited me to simultaneously pray in the Spirit for an unknown brother at the Eugene Mission in a funk, one that made my own seem more like a bad hair day. Propelled by a willingness born out of my own mounting desperation, Jesus privileged me to help Him bring truth and emotional peace to our friend Paul's wounded past and present.

As a by-product, Jesus left me in possession of my own healing Kiss from Heaven. Feeling refreshed, encouraged, full of joy, and a participant in the Lord's work again had ended my own funk in a heartbeat.

Look, I had known for years that praying for those who suffer will inevitably lighten our struggle. But how soon we forget. Have you ever pondered what prompted the Good Samaritan (Luke 10:25–37) to give his time, effort, and money to rescue a Jew, his sworn enemy? Could that Samaritan have been seeking a Kiss from Heaven but first needed to discover the Lord's way to steal one by ministering to his enemy (Luke 6:27–28)? Loving his sworn enemy like he did might have moved God's heart to pour out what that half-breed Samaritan needed, don't you think? We cannot know for certain but tucking that thought away in our spiritual toolboxes for our next funky day might encourage us to bless another as the first stop on the way to our own freedom and another Kiss from Heaven.

QUESTION: Where is the Kiss from Heaven from this God Story?

ANSWER: It is not uncommon for the Lord to move us into prayer for others without a clue we are doing so. What a wonderful blessing results for those who both minister and receive ministry at such times. This little episode is so ripe with Kisses from Heaven: Jesus preparing the way by my hours of desperate prayer, the exquisite timing and interaction as Paul and I met, the high degree of hunger for an encounter with the Lord within both of us, and an immediate willingness for him to open up to painful childhood trauma (showing he, too, was primed and ready for ministry). Then, as Jesus confirmed in the moment that Paul was meant to enter into that dialogue with me, Holy Spirit's truth quickly brought the presence of peace (not only in Paul's painful childhood trauma but also from his adult agoraphobia rooted in the same memory). Almost as a curtain call came Paul's rapid deliverance from the lifelong lie-based pain of worthlessness by way of a healing inner vision of Jesus imparting truth ("You will always matter to me") as Paul's father sold him as a child. Finally came the lovely metaphor of Holy Spirit saturating our ministry time with His presence during that downpour, and my own freedom as the Spirit used me as His vessel poured forth with life-altering ministry to Paul. As Jesus said, "And you shall know the truth, and the truth shall make you free" (John 8:32). Should we need any more proof, Christian, that the Lord is ready to open the prison doors in all our lives that we might see the goodness of God in the land of the living? No more proof needed by this blessed man.

A Fever of Unknown Origin (2011)

E mily and I needed out of Dodge. After an intense year of daily ministering inner healing at our home in Western Oregon and approaching burnout, we needed time to catch our collective breaths, so we were seeking a brief change of venue as the solution. Solitude in the desolate eastern part of our state seemed the perfect answer. Two days later, winding our way across the arid rolling plains into the rugged Wallowa Mountains near the town of Joseph, our search for solitude ended. Heralded by the muffled ring of a cell phone buried deep in the abyss of Emily's big black handbag wedged beneath the passenger's seat, her valiant effort to retrieve the call proved futile, but its voicemail was accessible and to the point. The message was from Mike Salley.

Mike and his wife, Lori, are co-founders and dynamic leaders of Show Mercy International, a Christian missionary organization developing a community, the "Field of Dreams," outside Kampala, Uganda. Holy Spirit had conceived this wonderful little work (not so little anymore) and birthed it through the Salley's obedience to provide housing, schooling, medical care, vocational training, and Christian spiritual growth for children orphaned by the African AIDS epidemic and sub-Sahara's scourge of malaria plaguing the continent. When you add kids from northern Uganda's squalor-ridden refugee settlements, along with the debilitating conditions arising from the nation's poverty itself, it is easy to recognize the need for their ministry.

Out of contact with Mike for months, we were quick to respond with a cell call of our own. Freshly returned from Africa with his family, he was apologetic for the intrusion but concerned for his wife, who was ill with a high fever, chills, headache, and lethargy. Mike was looking for advice, so I offered it. She had malaria until proven otherwise and needed medical evaluation for hospitalization.

Mike was understandably unconvinced. He reminded me that Show Mercy had conducted repeated missionary journeys to Uganda with hundreds of Christians for a decade, and not a single team member had contracted the disease. While I merely reinforced my recommendation, Mike continued: Not one member of an American family working full-time for the ministry in Kampala, Uganda's capital city, during those years had fallen ill to malaria. While holding my ground, Mike would wait to see how Lori fared overnight.

Our conversation had ended in limbo before I could confirm something of which I was confident: At that time, Show Mercy did not require team members to take malarial prophylaxis during their missionary trips. The near decade's absence of malaria among the non-profit's missionary teams appeared the basis for that decision. And why not? It was a compelling reason. While so, it also ignored the elephant in the living room—we were talking sub-Sahara Africa here, for decades a hotbed of the world's malaria epidemics where Uganda, itself, had one of the highest transmission rates of the disease found in any nation on Earth.

Admittedly, this was puzzling. If Lori ended up with malaria after all those years of disease-free missionary journeys, how that vicious killer suddenly reared its ugly head among the teams for the first time deserved—no, demanded—an answer.

Important as it was, the immediacy to focus on that answer all but vanished with Mike's cell call the following afternoon. Lori's confusion had increased alongside her rising temperature. So he had taken her to a small local hospital where doctors diagnosed her with malaria. Inaudibly but firmly Holy Spirit spoke: "Do not leave Lori in that hospital; take her to Portland." While entering a U-turn, I assured Mike we would arrive by late evening.

A Mounting Medical Dilemma

With heads spinning, Emily and I sped west on our own mission, backtracking our way across the eastern Oregon desert and over the Cascade Mountain range leading to home base in the Willamette Valley. Though not vast, my medical history with malaria would have been less memorable if not for a handful of stressful clinical experiences with that disease during my past mission trips to Asia. Pointedly, all those had manifested cerebral involvement. Mike reported Lori as confused. In no way was that good news.

Having completed an intense continuing education course in tropical medicine at the University of Colorado at Aurora (which centered on African disease) within the previous year, one salient point now surfaced from its content.

Resistance to the strain of falciparum malaria in sub-Sahara Africa to conventional pharmaceuticals was on the rise, and newer antimalarial medications, not yet approved for the United States by our Food and Drug Administration, were already part of African protocols. So, if Lori had falciparum malaria, the chance her disease would be resistant to readily available older-line drugs in America was highly probable. That thought was, well, unthinkable.

Why? Well, when cerebral complications arise, and patients with malaria do not receive effective medication, they commonly die. The brain does not like malaria; sadly, without proper care, it has little to say about it. Having Lori in the wrong hospital with a deadly brain disease and effective medication unavailable, could things get any worse?

Regrettably, yes. It was not only the disease and unavailable treatment that might hinder Lori's path to recovery; it could also be the local medical community itself. Physicians are, as a profession, highly resolute, diligent, and caring but often recalcitrant to unsolicited opinions or advice about treatment of their patients. It is rarely pride. Doctors cannot afford to be wrong; there is too much at stake. Seeking another physician's consultation is acceptable, even required, if that physician is a well-trained specialist. Acting on the advice from an unfamiliar or lesser credentialed doctor could breach good judgment or raise questions as to standard of care.

Despite my repeated short-term missionary experiences with malaria and years of practicing general and emergency medicine within miles of Lori's present location, I would not only be a stranger to the staff in her hospital but also an unknown and less-credentialed physician who lacked local privileges. The resistance I could face would be understandable but not acceptable; creating a potential logjam over treatment options for someone who was not my patient would be the last thing Lori needed. Yet I was already certain her life could rest in the balance. While I had hoped all my ruminating was merely overthinking this whole scenario, down deep, I knew better. One thing was certain: Holy Spirit's wisdom needed to run interference from now on.

Arriving at the hospital by 11:00 p.m., I could only gain access to Lori's chart by obtaining permission from both Mike and the nursing supervisor; the latter, per protocol, had to first talk to someone else, somewhere else. During that interval, what I saw was worrisome. To no surprise, Lori was taking oral doses of an historically accepted medication for treatment of falciparum malaria, now finding little success in Africa. Considering her present unchecked fever and reduced awareness, predictably due to the malarial parasites attacking her brain, Lori was showing signs of a downward course needing more effective treatment. I was concerned that the world's gold standard medication for cerebral malaria, presently available and effective against malaria in Africa, may yet be unavailable in the States. Who could not foresee that possibility as a major hurdle? Now, at 2:00 a.m., Lori's physician would arrive in five hours. That was an eternity. But I would be present.

A Tepid Encounter

Dawn found me slumped in the least hospitable of hospital chairs in a hallway thirty feet from Lori's room. Strategically positioned to intercept her attending physician during morning rounds worked as planned. The doctor was steady but unfamiliar with tropical disease. But then, who in a small city in Oregon could expect her to be? Predictably, our pointed discussion revealed that she had never treated malaria but would entertain my concerns, glean from my past clinical experience, and freely admit to her unfamiliarity with falciparum malaria's evolving resistance and the recent change in its treatment in Africa. Again, in her sphere of day-to-day practice, she little needed to know of that change—at least, until now.

Despite Lori's doctor's willingness to "listen," true to my preconceived concern, she could not "hear" and regrettably hesitated to refer Lori to a Portland facility. She did, to her credit, transfer her to the hospital's ICU to begin intravenous delivery of her present medication. That was a start. Not a great one, but a start. The doctor also agreed to consult with an infectious disease specialist from a nearby city. Unable to help her understand those wise decisions still missed the standard of care for advancing cerebral malaria, neither of us left that conversation feeling warm and fuzzy. Little better than a standoff was my take.

Holy Spirit had insisted that Lori transfer to Portland. The *why* for that was no longer an issue. The *how* undeniably was.

Another Iron in the Fire

The cell phone in my coat was ringing; it was a close friend of the Salleys who was caring for their two daughters. The younger had spiked a fever during the night and was ill. Requesting the Good Samaritan bring the little girl to the emergency department, the doctor on duty diagnosed a mild case of malaria and admitted her. Then, I hurried off to find Lori comatose in the ICU. It was a chilling sight. That we were still in limbo surrounding Lori's move to Portland provoked anxiety and was making me sick to my stomach.

The Last-Ditch Attempt

It was high noon when the infectious disease specialist from the neighboring city arrived. Strategically stationed, armed, and ready, but this time at the ICU nursing station, I understandably caught the doctor off guard by my ambush. Thank the Lord he was a professional and agreeable to listen. But would he hear? While quick to admit his inexperience with managing malaria, he was quicker to express a deep concern for Lori's unresponsive state.

Convinced this was my final opportunity to see Lori's life salvaged—and to enforce Holy Spirit's mandate—emboldened me. I became unwaveringly direct about Lori's almost certain and imminent death from cerebral malaria if he recommended continuing her medications in this hospital ill-equipped to treat her desperate condition. Using that tack felt like arm-twisting, borderline shameful, and frankly manipulative. Admittedly, it painted the specialist into a corner laced with an unspoken potential for litigation if things went further south—anything to convince him to move Lori to a Portland ICU. Anything. We could not afford another standoff.

Laying a Foundation

Earlier that morning, after my first failed attempt to have Lori transferred by her admitting physician, I had contacted a well-known and highly qualified infectious disease doctor at Providence St. Vincent Hospital in Portland. He had authored three scientific papers on falciparum malaria and was the treating physician on a long history of similar cases; he was also willing to take Lori as a patient. So, after sharing this information publicly in the ICU with the infectious disease physician and repeating my grave opinions like a gadfly, or better still, a piranha, I took my leave while hopefully still credible but not until confident that the specialist had genuinely heard and processed my arguments.

Thanking him cordially for his time while leaving the ICU, there was nothing more for me to do but wait and pray. It was up to the Lord; with absolute certainty, I knew what He wanted. Were we at another crossroads, another stalemate, or worse, that logjam I sought to avoid? The clock was no longer our ally. Instead, time looked like a turncoat and, though hard to admit, felt more like an enemy.

Breakthrough Moment

Crowded again into one of those hospital chairs that defy rest or prayer, within scant minutes, Lori's admitting physician, having consulted with the infectious disease specialist, came by to announce her decision to transfer Lori to the medical intensive care unit at the Oregon Health Sciences University (OHSU) in Portland. Having earlier reviewed the credentials of the infectious disease team at that medical school, I was convinced they were eminently qualified but without the history with falciparum malaria held by the St. Vincent's physician with whom I had spoken earlier.

Prepared to launch a salvo of reasons to dissuade her from referring Lori to OHSU but instead transport her to St. Vincent, Holy Spirit stopped me short with instructions to "leave well enough alone." More than surprised, but having long ago learned my lesson not to resist Him, I relented and went to seek Mike, who was already ambulance-bound for Portland.

With a pastor from our church, we set a course to OHSU in pursuit, while I was no more than marginally relieved at the recent turn of events. After all, what more could Portland offer? Still, this was Holy Spirit's plan; He wanted us in Portland, so something had to be up.

The Eleventh Hour

Lori made it, but had she made it in time? Mike, the pastor, and I gathered in the waiting room adjoining the OHSU intensive care unit, listening intently to a resident physician report on Lori's condition. This time, it was bone-chilling. She was in a deep coma secondary to cerebral malaria and not expected to survive the night. You could palpate the hush flooding the room. Hurriedly, the young physician pressed on. Looking to fill the void his grim news had created, he reported there might be a ray of hope: The FDA had recently given OSHU access to an experimental clinical protocol highlighted by a drug not yet approved in the States. Mike, however, would have to allow its use.

Cutting to the chase, the resident physician shared the "experimental" drug's generic name, and with it, my spirit leapt. It was the antimalarial now in routine use against drug-resistant falciparum malaria by African protocols with a high rate of success and the drug of choice recommended by the tropical disease course I had recently completed at the University of Colorado. Sharing that information with Mike and wholeheartedly encouraging him to give the staff permission to administer the drug as Lori's treatment captured Mike's attention as it had mine. As the good news sunk in, that resident physician's "ray of hope" came to life in Lori's husband's face.

Reduced to praising Jesus within my heart, now I understood why Holy Spirit, right out of the gate in eastern Oregon, was determined to have Lori transferred to Portland while having me hold my tongue about moving her to the St. Vincent facility. No one among us knew that OHSU was the single medical center in the Northwest outside Seattle allowed to administer that "experimental" drug. Holy Spirit had set the stage, the medication was now on a stat order, and the intensive care treatment team was standing by to administer it upon arrival.

An About-Face

Having seen cerebral malaria infections (accurately parasitic infestations of the brain) respond in the most dramatic and rapid ways when treated with proper medication gave me great hope. What lifted my confidence even higher was the memory of a young, comatose Cambodian teenager admitted with cerebral malaria early one morning years before in an Asian refugee camp who woke from her coma after treatment and was enjoying lunch by noon.

But for Lori, it was not to be so simple, for her enemy was poised to snatch defeat from the arms of a would-be victory. Mike, awakening at 5:00 a.m., spoke with the hospital only to learn his wife was not responding to the experimental drug and that her prognosis remained grave. Mike broke down in tears as he faced his wife's potential funeral and assuming care of his two daughters without Lori. Then, in his distress but without warning, Holy Spirit, as our faithful eleventh-hour God, arose in Mike to enter them into battle, taking authority in Christ over darkness, and, with a booming voice shaking the motel room, commanded Lori's illness to leave her in the mighty name of Jesus. After a rafter-shaking period of warfare, our valiant prayer warrior left for the hospital to find that Lori had indeed seized the victory he claimed in that motel room battle and, now set free from her coma, greeted her hero before beginning her own long and valiant road to recovery.

We watched Lori recover steadily from confusion until she finally surfaced free from the grip of that vicious disease like a butterfly free from her cocoon. Within months, she was her exuberant self, full of life, the love of Jesus, and again living life on purpose for Him. Within the year, to the best of my recollection, Mike, Lori, their two daughters, and a whole flock of fledgling missionaries once more headed to Kampala, Uganda, and their beloved Field of Dreams.

Postscript

The treating physicians may have (or not) verified the following hypothesis, but I would bet a year's wages it is spot-on. If you are an epidemiologist, you will love this anecdote. If you are not an epidemiologist (Google the definition), you will love it anyway. Here, we finally find the answer to that lingering question: Why, after all those years with no reported team cases of malaria in Uganda, did Lori (and one of her daughters and, later, another woman from the same trip) contract the disease—and all on the same trip?

Let us preface our way into the answer to this question by introducing a concept: the "sucker hole." (It is true; once an aviator, always an aviator.) A colloquialism familiar to the aviation community, this phrase aptly describes an opening where a pilot may spot blue sky or earth through a heavy overcast, a tempting hole that lures the aviator—without an instrument rating or proper instrumentation—into it in search of more favorable weather conditions. As the name implies, a "sucker hole" takes a pilot into worse weather without the skills or instrumentation to recover visual flight. Regrettably, the common result is to lose control of an airplane, often to a stall, followed by a spin, which ends in tragedy and loss of life.

Now to our answer arising from Lori's illness: For years, during day trips to the Field of Dreams (and other destinations), Show Mercy team members left their Kampala hotel rooms by midmorning for various rural sites but returned by late afternoon. That kept them safe from female Anopheles mosquitoes, the vectors for falciparum malaria, who feed on blood after dusk. On this mission trip, however, the team scheduled overnights at the not-yet-fully-mosquito-proofed sleeping quarters at the Field of Dreams. Unwittingly, those nights became figurative "sucker holes," a setup, and a snare abounding with inadequately protected spaces lacking repellant-applied mosquito netting, absence of full malarial medicinal prophylaxis by team members, and the proximity of a nearby village reservoir of malaria.

None of the above conditions posed a threat during daylight hours over the previous years, as team members moved safely among local Anopheles mosquitoes hidden away from the dehydrating heat of a day's tropical sun. Nor were those mosquitoes a threat after sundown since the teams were reliably retired by the later afternoon to their Kampala hotel. But now, as dusk crept into the little Field of Dreams, an unperceived risk arrived as the final but most essential condition to complete an equation for calamity.

Exiting daily hiding places, squadrons of female Anopheles mosquitoes allied themselves with those previously inconsequential conditions (inadequate external protection, absent internal prophylaxis, and a proximate reservoir of malaria) to ensure unopposed transmission of malarial parasites from that nearby village via those flying hosts to three unsuspecting and soundly sleeping team members, one who would need a God-breathed and orchestrated rescue from death's doorstep,

Happily, all three victims on that trip not only survived but no further cases of malaria have appeared over a full decade since Show Mercy buttoned down those sleeping quarters, protected all team members with malaria prophylaxis, and reduced the incidence of malaria in that nearby village. And guess what? There is now an operational medical facility on the Show Mercy site. Don't all things work together for good for those who love God and are called according to His purposes (Rom. 8:28)?

What number of Kisses from Heaven did Holy Spirit freely distribute while solving this complex Agatha-Christie-like whodunit to assure our hero a healing and put her purposeful life back on course? Count 'em. Then count 'em again. Does the goodness of God and Holy Spirit's commitment to never leave or forsake but instead walk us to the other side of calamity get any better than this nail-biter? We should ask Lori for that answer. So glad we can, aren't you?

QUESTION: Where is the Kiss from Heaven from this God Story?

ANSWER: Of all the God Stories in our past where Holy Spirit has spoken, this cliff-hanger presented more obstacles and needed greater faith to bring them under our feet. Driving from the far reaches of Oregon's eastern high desert to the lowlands of the Willamette Valley with instructions to move Lori to Portland, I knew Jesus would have to make a way where there was no way with no guarantee that the care in that city would be any more effective. That was true as we knew it. All we had was Holy Spirit's command to depend upon (as if that should not be enough).

Honestly, we ran entirely on faith that when reaching our destination, He would bring about His good, acceptable, and perfect will (healing). Of course, when our hero arrived in Portland, Jesus once again revealed Himself to be the eleventh-hour God He so often becomes—when faith to move mountains reduced to mustard seeds still takes us across the finish line. None of us knew in advance that the only effective drug on the entire globe against drug-resistant falciparum malaria was the subject of an experimental study authorized by the FDA in that Portland hospital, the single Oregon facility where the drug was available and legally administered. So reaching that elusive city in time, having that drug available, and Mike's willingness to use it became the final obstacles overcome for Lori's healing to begin.

"Faith is the substance of things hoped for, the evidence of things not seen. For by it the elders obtained a good testimony" (Hebrews 11:1–2, NKJV). Now, Mike and Lori (Oh, won't you include us too?) have a Kiss from Heaven and a marvelous God Story as a testimony to the goodness of God in the land of the living to pay forward. "Freely you received," said our Savior, "freely give" (Matt. 10:8). Lori, Mike, Emily, and I have done our parts, Christian. Maybe it's your turn to share this story for His glory.

A Christmas Journey (2015)

Having barely survived the first year and poised to head full steam into a second as the president of a homeowners' association in Texas, I found myself so numb, cold, and disappointed with a select number of humankind—on whose behalf I had spent twenty-five hundred hours of volunteer labor, twelve months of insomnia, and likely set a new record for high-stress cortisol hormone levels—that I needed a way out of my cistern of joylessness. "No good deed goes unpunished," quoted my son, the lawyer. Believe you me, Christian, Jeremiah had nothing on this old man.

Awaking one December night during that siege, I puzzled how to "give" my way out of my inner sadness and turmoil. Three thoughts came one after the other. The first was to bring Christmas to a struggling Mexican family I visited earlier at the end of a deteriorating road but three miles from our home. Sadly, further investigation proved that the family had moved. Next was for Emily and me to personally pay off the delinquent HOA dues owed by a hurt and angry owner struggling financially in the grips of a nasty divorce. That was doable. Finally, we severely limited our own gift exchange to, instead, cruise the inner-city streets of Brownsville near the international border with Mexico on a Merry Christmas morning, taking with us a stash of twenties to distribute among people whom Holy Spirit might wish to bless.

Midmorning found Emily and me leaving a twenty-dollar tip with our now happiest of waitresses at the only IHOP open for business in town on that Christmas Day. Our reconnaissance by car then began. Within minutes, we spotted an animated Hispanic man in his early twenties hawking newspapers on what was normally a busy street corner. That morning, while folks were sharing gifts elsewhere, to no surprise, that corner's traffic was slowed to a trickle. Emily and I both voiced the identical question in unison: "Don't you think Holy Spirit wants that young man to receive a Kiss from Heaven?"

Now laughing in unison, we scurried around the block in light traffic to approach His target. As the car slowed, the young man moved toward us in anticipation of Emily rolling her window down to request a paper. Taking it, she said, "Merry Christmas, God bless you, keep the change." Holy smokes, you would have thought that man had won the Texas lottery.

What do I mean? Well, first, he took an unsteady step backward while performing the sign of the cross, followed by bursting forth with abundant thanks again and again to Emily, Jesus, and all creation. On and on, his waves of gratitude washed over us. Oh, the healing warmth of it all. In a blessed instant, I felt my cold, dead heart embrace that gratitude and spring to life. Tears, the first in months, took over, quickly tumbling off my chin to soak a thirsty shirt downstream. Flying to the joyous possibilities, my mind went to a little child receiving an unexpected Christmas gift, an unplanned holiday dinner, or perfume for his sweetheart. It was almost concussive how that gift struck each one of us, like a love bomb going off next to the car, its shrapnel penetrating each of us with inexpressible joy.

Wasn't my logical mind saying, "Hey, it is twenty dollars, closer to eighteen after the paper. What is the deal? Why the overreaction?" But I got it! And my heart got it! Who would have known? The young man had clearly been desperate, drowning in uncontrollable circumstances for lack of funds. For whatever reason, Jesus had thrown him a life ring. Suddenly, he had his head above water and could breathe again. "Oh, Jesus, so could I."

All he could say was, "Thank you, thank you, thank you." I could say nothing, absolutely nothing, because I was ruined, absolutely ruined. Glancing at Emily, she was absolutely ruined too. Also, hooked. Oh yes, we were both hooked. So, after blessing our young friend, we parted and headed deeper into the older section of the city. Public works had widened selected streets in Old Town but avoided others.

Rows of houses were elderly and dilapidated, interrupted only to wedge gas stations or mom-and-pop businesses into the gaps. Soon, we saw few, if any, white folks. Then none. The streets became hollow corridors, void of any activity, except for an occasional pedestrian aimlessly heading who knows where on that sundrenched morning. *Christmas morning*, I thought, *shouldn't feel so lonely and be crawling with so much inactivity*. It was as if Old Town had taken the day off.

"Where," we kept asking the Lord, "are the folks who are meant to receive Your blessings?" At that very moment, there came a middle-aged Hispanic man making his way toward us but on the opposite side of the street. His head, covered with an aged, faded blue baseball cap, hung down atop a body stooped and slowed beyond its years. Both Emily and I could taste the despair. Jesus welled up with the compassion that only He can feel for the broken, while the Spirit within celebrated, expecting what was on the way. For the second time that morning, we took a quick tum around the block to intercept the entire reason we were there.

He was still shuffling along. Unintentionally, we startled him by pulling alongside the curb. Undeterred by the surprise, he took the three steps needed to reach Emily's open window, clearly ready to help us, while his face showed no curiosity as to what we wanted. Truthfully, there was not much at all readable; rather, he appeared somewhere else. The twenty-dollar bill brought him back. He placed the sincerity of his "oh no, no, no!" in jeopardy by unmasking an enormous grin, a tsunami of joy engulfing and now lighting up his entire face. That grin betrayed not only his words but an outstretched palm gesturing like a mime trying to push the twenty dollars away. What a living paradox! Here was a proud, capable man in distress but still striving to keep his dignity and independence. Simultaneously, there was the truth: relief mixed with joy from a grateful heart for an unexpected blessing escaping every pore of his being.

"Yes," Emily countered, "the Lord wants you to have this; please receive it." Those words he understood. His Master's wish was for him to take the gift. With that epiphany, his gratitude simply overcame his pride, and a new willingness to receive the blessing bubbled forth as a cloudburst of heartfelt love laced with thank you after thank you. Life had changed. It was Christmas. Then, blessing both of us, he straightened up and slipped away, confident that today Jesus had chosen him to bless. What could be more precious? Our tears were once more flowing, and our hearts undone again, ravished by the merciful love of God. Basking in His goodness, it took a brief time to catch our emotional breaths. But you can bet it was not too long before we were composed enough to move on to more of the same.

More of the same, I tell you, took no time. Scurrying around another corner of opportunity, we stopped abruptly to avoid hitting a man formally dressed in black, buzzed, and half falling off the curb just ahead. The Lord gave us clearance as Emily reached for another twenty. Our man in black's on-board alcohol blunted his surprise and gratitude. With closer exam, he was a taller gentleman, thin with an aquiline nose and a face leathered by years in the sun. Outside these surroundings, you might have assumed him a politician, a banker, or a successful businessperson. Sadly, in this lonely place, he was like any other soul trapped in a cistern of addiction.

Now, you may ask why, when we realized this gift could buy cheap wine, we chose not to withhold it? Well, long ago, I set aside that argument plus others I would offer when Jesus repeatedly asked us to give hard-earned cash to folks trapped by the grip of substances. "What is that to you?" Jesus would tirelessly ask before I came to understand His point—that an addicted man must eventually eat. "And if that twenty dollars goes for cheap wine and his pain disappears for a short season before he eats, maybe, just maybe, it will give him time to remember when you, without any strings attached or condemnation, reminded him: 'Here, celebrate this wonderful day. The Lord loves you, wants to bless you, save you from this difficult life, and be your best friend.'"

With that, Jesus would continue, "The pain may stay away just a little while longer and show that in my sphere of influence, love places every man's value at eye level with every other man's. You know that Father God's mercy longs to see every man getting not the condemnation he deserves for his sin but, instead, not only forgiveness but a blessing, eternal life (to know God and the Christ that He has sent, John 17:3), which he does not deserve at all.

"Shouldn't every man knit together by Me understand this? And, furthermore, when I forgive a man's sin, and he surrenders to me as Lord, in Father's eyes that man becomes holy, blameless, and beyond reproach (Col. 1:22). Then he shall know the truth, and that truth shall set him free. No man can be bound by any chain when he knows his freedom in Me, his Savior." It was not the first time, nor would it be the last that I heard that inner argument as Jesus offered eternal life in a creative but comfortable way to His chosen.[8]

Lost in the backstreets now, very few looks we received from the locals were festive. On one corner of the lot was a decaying building with an equally decaying parking lot up front—and, okay, a decaying old truck parked nearby. In harmony with everything else

---

[8] Understandably, various drug and alcohol rehabilitation centers whom we support in full measure would object to our approach to giving cash to addicts. We stand with them unless Holy Spirit so instructs which, though infrequent and not uniform, demands our obedience. Otherwise, we give our treasure to support drug and alcohol rehabilitation centers' policies without qualification.

surrounding him, a shabbily dressed man was squatting alongside the vehicle on his haunches, sound asleep with his head hovering over what I assumed were his personal effects enclosed in a dirty pillowcase. Though sleeping, he was on guard, a skillset learned to preserve the necessities and the few treasures that traveled with him. *How can anyone sleep like that?* was my thought. There was no time to receive an answer to that question, for the man arose from his guarded sleep, quickly took the money offered without hesitation, and showing his appreciation by smiling and thanking us for the gift, grabbed his belongings and left. That coordinated move was to the point, cut and dried, and as if he had been through this uncomfortable but regrettably necessary process before. This man, too, looked, spoke, and behaved out of place as if he did not belong in this decayed setting. Pondering the moment brought an epiphany: "Here in this place, poverty and addictions are the great equalizers." What I had not seen for so long was that some of those trapped in this prison without bars were as educated, talented, and skilled as the stable, clean, and sober folks we rub shoulders with daily. I did not like how that felt because I saw what it meant: Were it not for the mercy and grace of God helping us to transcend unintended bad choices or innocent mistakes in our own lives, we'd need to make room for the rest of us in this purgatory assigned to the addicted, the afflicted, and the needy.

That fact ringing so true in my life at the time and challenging my faith daily was based on the consequences of a situation with our HOA that could potentially threaten (but eventually did not) our future. Pushing into my eighth decade with few current skills to support us left me stranded with this understanding: When said and done, Emily's and my entire dependence on the mercy and grace of God did not differ from that offered the folks surrounding us in this place. When stripped of all else, Jesus will eventually reveal Himself as the sole refuge, source of provision, and only protection for the whole of humanity. That may take thought, dear one, and even more prayer to digest.

Underway again, the town morphed into a section two blocks in length with nary a parking spot unoccupied and what most people would be prone to call a traffic jam. Really, it was more a people jam. Folks from adjacent crowded sidewalks were pouring into the street, busy chatting with drivers crawling along with no clear destination in sight. Hordes of others were entering and exiting dozens of stores, clearly welcoming business. It was a beautiful slice of Mexican Christmas culture, a bustling day of activity and friendship—and all happening in the space of a soccer field. Happy faces, greetings, laughter, and unrestrained decibels of festival music filled the air.

Once having inched through the clutter, chaos, and charm of it all, we slipped back into a noticeably quieter part of the commercial area, one with stores barred tight as prisons where pedestrians bore their entire life's possessions on their backs or secured to the elderly frames of bicycles. It was surreal. One block away was prosperity and Christmas cheer but, in this place, once again, poverty and despair. Somewhere along our journey, Emily and I saw we were living on purpose that day. Our little unannounced missionary trip was touching one heart at a time and bringing the true message of Christmas from the heart of Jesus to those left out of this world's celebration—but whom He wished to include in His.

From somewhere came a gentleman, an octogenarian at the very least, pedaling a bicycle rivaling his age and loaded with all his cherished goods safely stowed in bundles lashed to his handlebars and behind his seat. With the enthusiasm of a teenager, he stopped, dismounted, and headed for a couple of bills dangling from Emily's fingers. He, like his predecessors, was excited, smiling ear to ear and grateful for his all-too-unexpected Christmas present. After a plethora of "gracias," the only words among a waterfall we could understand, we parted when he moved on.

Across the street, a growing group of men gathered about the entrance to a busy tavern were watching our exchange with interest.

When they moved toward us in force, it prompted us to close the car's windows. Hastily pulling away from the oncoming throng, I heard Holy Spirit say, "Money serves many but masters others." We kept a keen eye on that disquieting band of men slowly shrinking in the center of our rearview mirrors. Does this sudden departure betray our mission? Didn't Jesus occasionally escape, disguise himself, or change His destination when things became tense? Read your Bible.

Approaching the bus station, we saw this man waiting on a bench. Swinging yet another U-turn, he stared at us through it. Unlike that day's earlier encounters, this peculiar person was slow to rise and had somewhat of a questioning and even suspicious look on his face as he carefully, even hesitantly, approached our car.

Emily held out money, and, with no fanfare or thank you, he took it, only to return without a word to his bench. His behavior betrayed him as one of our schizophrenic brethren wandering city streets in this day of independent living by medicated mentally ill patients. Whether the man felt happiness with his gift was less important, Holy Spirit reminded us, than how Jesus felt about it. "To the extent that you did it to one of these brothers of Mine, *even* the least *of them*, you did it to Me" (Matt. 25:40). Seems like, I mused, we had given Jesus a birthday present.

Continuing, we found ourselves among more familiar surroundings; they were streets we had traveled earlier. In this inner-city maze, we had become lost woodsmen looking for a way out of a forest of buildings by traveling in a circle.

And, lo and behold, there in our little urban jungle, traveling in the direction opposite from the first time we met him, was one of our earlier contacts. Emily said, "We only gave him a twenty; let's give him an extra twenty and another one to give away." So, once again, around the block we circled in time to intercept our quarry at another quiet intersection. We were getting good at this when I hollered, "Sir," and he turned around. "Sir," I continued, "we forgot to give you this gift."

Well, sure enough, here came the "no, no, no!" with the palm stretched out, but this time with the other hand pressed against his chest as if trying to catch his breath.

"Yes," I said, "this time, you keep one and give the other away." Well, he lit up like the Yuletide-decorated lamppost standing beside him. Then he took his turn to say yes and to come to a rapid agreement with our request. Not one yes but yes in multiples poured forth while his head bobbed in rhythm with each affirming word. Becoming the giver of the gift lifted his joy to a crescendo. Later, in retrospect, we wondered if we had been entertaining angels unawares that day. Reliving the whole scene ruined us again. Why, you would think it was Christmas.

Postscript

Years ago, Holy Spirit gave away this nugget: "If you are struggling, go minister to someone else who is suffering." It has been necessary to relearn that lesson repeatedly over time, but guess what? It has never failed. So here Emily and I were all body slammed over our HOA struggles and figuring, "Let's go find people like us who are suffering." So we did, and what an otherworldly period of blessing we had entered. The Lord has etched those gracious and grateful faces into our collective memories for a lifetime. What a complete release into joy our Christmas missionary journey had become.

So, how are you doing, Bubba? Are you feeling a little long in the tooth, sick and tired of being sick and tired, or your get up and go has got up and gone? Have your sweet dreams turned to nightmares, your rich uncle died and left you nothing but disappointment, or your best friend let you know he is not? Are you feeling less down in the dumps and more like the dump itself? If so, Emily and I have a recommendation: Go, find your face in the faces of the crowd around you; then, bless that face as if it were your own and expect nothing other than a big Christmas Kiss from Heaven from Jesus Himself.

QUESTION: Where is the Kiss from Heaven from this God Story?

ANSWER: The late Korean pastor David Yonggi Cho once shared this story: Early on, his fledgling church plant was struggling to grow. I am not sure the reason, nor was he at the time. One night during the offering, a poverty-stricken widow brought her sole possession in life to the Lord, a tin cup used for food and drink. We are reminded of the poor widow giving all she had (Luke 21:2–4)—two copper coins to show her love for God by giving out of her poverty. In Cho's story, the woman went beyond poverty; she had no money, so she gave away her very source of life as love to the Lord. That gift broke the shackles off the congregation's hearts and pocketbooks as the church flourished into the largest congregation in the world, approaching one million souls.

That Christmas Sunday, Emily and I needed some shackles broken off our hearts. Giving pennies or Tupperware never crossed our minds, but we had a bunch of hard-earned twenties. So we set out to give our way out of our shackles by loving those who could not shed their own without some cold, hard cash given in love on that beautiful Christmas Day. And you know, we are pretty sure it worked out for those folks. We know it did for us. And don't we all know how happy Jesus gets when we give to the least of His brethren, taking it as our giving to Him at the same time (Matt. 25:40)? Whoa, and on His birthday too. Happy Birthday, Jesus.

A Life Well-Lived (2018)

A good name is better than good oil and the day of death
is better than the day of one's birth.
—*Ecclesiastes 7:1*

We apologize if this rambling comes across as mystical, sappy, or even unhinged, but Emily and I, two of his beloveds among a multitude, cannot grasp the reality he has passed. That he is no longer with us exceeds the inconceivable because he has always been with us, even now. That is not doublespeak, dear one, for absence is the irrevocable dead-end and full realization of a passing; at that point, someone is gone for good and inaccessible.

Yet Pastor Hubert Robert "Bob" Curry's passing is not an absence, for the man lingers with us, steadfastly refusing to vacate the hearts of those whom he has always loved and who continue to love him. For that multitude, Bob will forever be an indelible friend, father, and mentor who is but a thought away, a thought guaranteed to access us not only comfort but this confidence: It is truly within reach of mortals to love and experience one another well beyond the veil.

Pastor Bob Curry will always be to all his "kids" such a big loving man, both in body and Spirit, bigger than life to those who know him, and one of those Godsmeared seekers of His glory who, even if passing through a person's life as a brief whirlwind (as was often the case), would be certain to slow down long enough to Velcro himself to anyone with a willing heart. So privileged are we, still touched, even branded, by his Jesus-life-well-lived.

About "Glorious"

Pastor Bob and yours truly shared six mission trips over the years, the last in the 1990s. Those adventures were all "glorious," a word Bob used often but beyond my grasp of its existential meaning. For example, the man of God would boldly say that Holy Spirit reliably made "glorious" visits to those who tarried after 2:00 a.m. Early on, I had no understanding of what that meant or whether that intrepid statement was factual or fanciful, mostly because I consistently tucked myself away under the feathers way before that absurd hour.

Predictably, each of those dead-of-night gatherings, which reliably invaded the wee morning hours (where my absence was conspicuous), would welcome the presence of God falling gloriously upon a remnant of insomniacs earnestly holding fast in faith of His coming. Listening to the ensuing morning's lavish reports, I would privately lament for having been ingloriously sleeping the entire time in an upstairs bedroom ten feet overhead the whole glorious event. Akin, wasn't it, to the boys sacked out in the Garden of Gethsemane while Jesus passionately sought Father's presence just feet away? Who does that?

Grievously, we remember those who ignore history are bound to repeat it.

One can now grasp why I was for a time denied Pastor Bob's existential understanding surrounding the word glorious, which always conveyed to my dear brother a close encounter of a God kind and a manifestation of His presence. Those of us who knew Bob came to treasure the hunger he instilled in us for the glorious and the resolve to overcome distraction and forsake the lure of comfort when promised tangible encounters with Holy Spirit. Finally, Pastor Bob instilled the tenacity to pursue those encounters relentlessly until we found Him. "Seek them to find Him!" History may decide this simple axiom to be Pastor Bob Curry's crowning legacy to us all.

In this and our following books, Pastor Bob is a cameo and then a highlight, which illustrates God's amazing favor on his life. All are testaments to a man and his abiding "John Chapter 15" relationship with Holy Spirit. If you allow me, I have but one final "glorious" Bob Curry tale worth sharing here. It is just another demonstration of how the Lord is so kind to His kids when they are Bob Curry's kids too.

Following Meriwether

Emily and I had not been to the Northwest as a couple for five years. It was time to visit friends and family, and that would include our brother Bob. It was the summer of 2018 and no season to be at the southernmost tip of the great State of Texas, which exalts ambient temperatures to poster child status—to the joy of our nation's highest echelon of global warming (sorry, climate change) enthusiasts. Being quick to routinely celebrate that dubious honor, an equally dubious array of Texas officialdom hosts a fully government-funded week of festivities for themselves along with a dozen cherry-picked-not-so-proud Texas elite from the Peoples' Republic of Austin. Okay, none of that is true. But it feels like it could be true . . . and soon will become true if them interlopers from the Left Coast keep-a-coming to "California-ize" our sacred wide-open spaces under starry skies above.

Okay, where were we? Oh, we were in Dallas when the following news arrived from a shared missionary friend in Georgia, Pastor Phil Freeman, with whom we had not spoken in two decades: Brother Bob Curry had entered a hospital in Eugene, Oregon, where physicians gave him from four to fourteen days to live.

Our GPS presented us with a thirty-two-hour trip; that would be four ten-hour days if we included frequent pit stops and mandatory one-hour naps, both capitulations to the incessant demands of my seventy-nine-year-old frame. People say that when you have driven a mile in North Texas, you have seen North Texas. Let us be flat (pardon the pun) honest and call that one-half mile. Then come Oklahoma, New Mexico (only if you miss your right turn into Kansas, which we did), Colorado, Wyoming, Utah, Idaho, and, finally, Oregon herself.

One reaches that latter destination only after days of grinding-dye-straight, never-ending freeway driving across a not-so-fruited plain to an eventual surrender, without warning or choice, to an eternal roller-coaster ride through sometimes verdant but all-times vertiginous mountain majesty. Only by abusing more words could I spruce up those everlasting hours of monotony or describe the never-ending array of tedious turns and ear-popping altitude changes or the way too much driving for any old guy on any old day that separated us from our quest. Day after day, it was taking too long; we were legitimately concerned. Would we make it to Eugene in time?

But harken (harken: a word to get your undivided attention) to this earful.

During our sleepover in an Idaho La Quinta motel, I had a dream. I rarely recall dreams (actually, but three in my entire life), but that night was to be different.

Pastor Bob Curry was lying in a hospital bed in severe respiratory distress. From his chest came an assortment of rumbles, gurgles, and wheezes as he struggled to capture each precious breath. Suddenly, he coughed with such force as to thrust himself into a sitting position, where racked with paroxysm after paroxysm, he was losing a battle to remain conscious. Then it happened: with one final momentous, memory-making cough, a foreign body approximating the size of a small lima bean jettisoned from his mouth onto the bedsheet covering his legs. Instantly, Bob sat erect and, breathing effortlessly, a smile consumed his relieved face. I awoke in a quasi-paradoxical state of joy and empathic relief.

We Arrive, But to What?

Well, Pastor Bob was not in that Eugene hospital. Had he passed on? That was worrisome. Then the admissions folks, after a frantic search, revealed a discharge but no one knew to where. Really? Really! So we traveled twenty miles south the following morning to his home in Cottage Grove to visit his wife, Joan, who, following a harrowing motor vehicle accident earlier on, found herself in the hospital. Given her cell number, we reached her eldest daughter in the very hospital we had visited earlier. During our conversation, we discovered Pastor Bob's whereabouts; he had transferred to a rehabilitation facility in Creswell, Oregon, a town ten miles away that we had passed through twice within the hour. "Eureka, Holmes, in a roundabout way, I believe we've found our man."

If nursing homes were lovely, that Creswell facility fit the bill. Well-staffed with a welcoming receptionist, engaging nurses and aides, it took little time to be at Bob's side. As his physician for a decade, it was sad to see him in this disheveled state. The last few years had not been kind. Asleep but hard at work to move any air to his lungs, he woke easily to fix his eyes on us. To Bob, we were strangers. Emily moved to his left side, I to his right. She opened the conversation, which rapidly distilled to, "Do you remember Doctor Woodworth?"

At first, Bob, his face etched with confusion, paused; then, a smile stole the confusion. "Yes, I do remember. Where is he?" Emily pointed at me, and Bob asked, "Is that you, my brother?" (Later, we found diabetes had stolen his sight.)

Smiling, I answered, "It is, Pastor Bob." Now, he was beaming at us both.

Beaming aside, Bob was in serious shape. It was a malignancy, a cancer in his chest. His respirations were severely labored, while his words seized any small opportunity to escape through the decibels of distressed breathing. We talked sparingly. He was overly exhausted, slipping into sleep for minutes at a time.

Rallying at one point, he moved Emily to his right and myself to his left. Holding our hands, he prayed faintly, dozing intermittently over the next half an hour. With permission and praying silently, Emily anointed our dear brother's feet with oil. Before leaving, we laid hands upon him, each giving him a holy kiss, as his wish.

We took our leave sooner than expected. Bob was feeble, so very weak, in significant distress, and clearly failing. It was heart-wrenching to see our day's brief time together wind down in such a way—hollow, unfulfilling, and unfinished. There had been so much more to share, so many old times to reminisce, and so many endearments and prayers left unsaid. Intending to return at an earlier hour on another day, we hoped Bob might be more alert, but our hearts feared otherwise. Pulling out of the nursing home's parking lot, Emily and I puzzled over that fading Idaho night's dream. Who knew? Perhaps it had been that before-bed Idaho pizza?

Doing the Right Thing When It Is Too Hard

It was not a decision easily reached. We preferred not to visit Creswell again. More from senses of duty, respect, and love, days later, Emily and I made our way from Portland to Bob's nursing home. We knew there was little chance he would be on the mend but a much better one on his way to or already in the arms of Jesus. Little leeway or much for us to look forward to, was there? The visit was more out of seeking closure with our dear friend and brother. Earth, without him on it, would never be the same.

Struggling to enter the nursing home, here came that warm welcome from the staff. This time, the greeting felt discordant, out of place, and almost inappropriate alongside the potential outcome and heaviness resting upon this visit. The staff's well-intended greeting received little acknowledgment beyond our bland "Morning."

Preoccupied and holding our collective breaths, we focused on the approach to Bob's room, steadily morphing into an unnerving and unavoidable black hole. Our hands tightened in each other's as we approached the doorway.

Inadequately armored against disappointment and loss and fighting to stay intentional, we stumbled on, guarded only by uncertainty. How often in my life had I made the journey to a dying patient's bedside? It had never been easy. That morning, it was beyond difficult. Crossing the threshold to Bob's room, whatever was to come would be a life-impacting event.

As predicted, that crossing became an unavoidable life-impacting event. Pastor Hubert Robert "Bob" Curry was still in his room and, as so, still confined to his bed. This time, however, he was no longer a prisoner to it but sitting bolt upright, feet dangling over its side, close-shaven, every hair on his head in place, smiling ear to ear, vibrant, vocal, and breathing without a decibel of complaint from those until now irascible lungs.

The whole surreal scenario quickly unraveled into a "What? Whoa! Wait a minute!" moment for both Emily and me. Oh my, we were more than a little taken aback, befuddled, and shocked but even more so overcome with an unexpected tsunami of unspeakable joy. Hold on, world, Father God was up to something wonderful! Predictably, Emily's and my first questions were identical and, as if choreographed, in unison, "Bob, what has happened to you?"

"Well, kids," Brother Bob, now an all-star shortstop deftly fielding our questions and ready to sling a zinger to first base, reliably fired back: "Last night, I was having an awful time breathing with terrible pain in my chest. At one point, I began to cough so hard that I had to sit up in bed to breathe at all. Still, I could not catch any air and wondered if I was going to pass out. Then, suddenly, right in the middle of that huge coughing spell, something flew from my mouth onto the bedsheet covering my legs. The pain instantly disappeared, and I could breathe freely again and have been fine ever since."

Oh my! Didn't Emily and I exchange the biggest and broadest smiles across that hospital bed. Lo and behold, our Idaho pizza dream was alive and well in Creswell, after all.

"Oh, ye of little faith," Holy Spirit might have murmured had we been listening and not so consumed by the moment.

Fellowship

Oh, the glorious hours of fellowship that followed, every one of them shared with Bob's younger brother, David, and nursing staff whom our patient intermittently and enthusiastically "ordered" off the floor to share another of his spellbinding missionary tales. Spending hours reminiscing over our common journeys during those bountiful years from the Philippines to Finland to Romania and beyond, the Lord reminded us of all the perils He surmounted, miracles He supplied, and meetings He conducted under the glorious hand of Holy Spirit. So many precious spiritual souvenirs we had lost or forgotten became unearthed and restored to treasured memories. How we laughed, teared up, prayed, and rejoiced over those glorious bye-gone encounters.

How great was the praise to our God! How wonderful our renewed love for each other! How kind and full of unfathomable mercies was this respite that Father had created, carved out, and set aside for all of us to share with Him! Then, all too soon, it was time for our fellowship to end. Bob needed rest. So we prayed, embraced, shared holy kisses, exchanged ever-so-reluctant good-byes, and then parted, leaving our dear brother in the care of his Great Physician.

A Change of Residence

Days later, we returned; had the nursing home discharged Pastor Bob? They had not. Entering his room, we found him in no distress, resting comfortably but with no response or fanfare. Medical folks would diagnose his state as obtunded, even comatose. Emily and I felt he had entered Father's rest, and without question, we were on holy ground with Bob's homecoming at hand. It was as if he were already at Heaven's gates. That was no surprise, for the Lord had given us a moving inner vision earlier on our trip where those gates were all that restrained a multitude of familiar shining faces, full of anticipation, belonging to those who loved our brother, preceded him to Heaven, and awaited his coming home (Heb. 12:1). We prayed and left to meet good friends.

Hours later, Reverend Hubert Robert Curry left to meet his best friend (Ps. 116:15).

Postscript

You are not aware that the Lord had been prompting us for upwards of a year to contact Bob. I felt as though He wanted us to make one more trip wherever the Spirit wished to lead him. That could have been around the world or around the block. Anywhere or nowhere. Mattered little. Sadly, more sadly than I wish to confess, the things of this world choked out Holy Spirit's leading for us. What did we forgo that the Lord had planned? Only He knows.

Yet Jesus is so forgiving and merciful. Think about it this way: Had the Lord not prompted that Georgia missionary (with whom we had not visited in fifteen years) to contact us, or had Holy Spirit not given and then brought to life that pizza dream to open a window of time for us to share our love with Bob during his final days, how we would have grieved over losing those precious moments preceding his passing. Instead, the blessing was ours to be there for him and with him, to rekindle friendships with his wife, Joan, his children, David, Bob's extended family, and, as always, to be lifted up in fellowship with our mutual Best Friend.

Pastor Bob's memorial service was, well, repetitious in a glorious way. Love, love, love, love, and more love from all who knew him. Loving words and loving acts. Only pure love poured out upon an old friend who, had he been physically present, would have multiplied that love to each one of us in return.

The Bible states, "Let the elders who rule well be considered worthy of double honor" (1 Tim. 5:17). Now consider Pastor Bob, by then tucked into Heaven among that glorious cloud of witnesses (Heb. 12:1), watching us pay him double honor, predictably from a front row seat between Mom Curry (a giant of the faith herself) and Jesus (the author of faith Himself). Didn't that day's celebration end up a Kiss from Heaven that far surpassed our humble brother's fondest dreams?

See you in His time, dear friend.

QUESTION: Where is the Kiss from Heaven from this God Story?

ANSWER: Had Missionary Phil Freeman, intermittent co-laborer like me with Pastor Bob Curry over the years, not had the mercy to call us, Emily and I would have driven to the Northwest without knowing Bob was terminally ill and likely missed our time with him. But Pastor Phil did call when we, unknowingly, were already on our way to the Northwest. Then, had it not been for the puzzling "pizza dream" in the Boise, Idaho, motel haunting us into a return visit to Bob's nursing home (after our initial disappointing one), we might have foregone that second trip from Portland altogether. But that dream kept niggling us and would not let us alone. Then, an inner vision of a grand welcoming throng awaiting Bob at the gates of Heaven finally convinced us that Bob must still be in the land of the living and to no longer delay our return to his nursing home. The rest is history: Bob's real-life reenactment of that pizza dream, a bigger-than-life renewal of our relationship, reliving our most memorable missionary moments, and allowing Holy Spirit time to minister the love of Jesus among us for an entire afternoon. Then, with closure and sealed by holy kisses all around, we departed for Portland and, soon thereafter, Bob for his grand welcome and reunion at those pearly gates.

Afterthoughts

I, Caleb, the storyteller and eyewitness in this book, am concerned that I have not adequately conveyed to my readers an unshakeable understanding that Father is unrelenting to reveal His active presence in our lives, to keep us engaged in our relationship with Him, and that His inexpressible goodness and kindness is always working to exchange His beauty for the ashes in our lives (Isa. 61:3)—but often on the sly. And, wouldn't you know, the glorious events in this book so often happened without our being aware of His heavenly hand until He had departed with it? Truthfully, we had prayed for none of these "Kisses from Heaven" (well, unless you consider the sputtering faithless plea I uttered during His rescue of my daughter's little gold earring or the unrecognizable spiritual glossolalia before the trip to the Eugene mission). They were all unsolicited surprises, lacked any advanced warning, always targeted someone in need (sometimes us), ended by bringing the Lord glory, and, almost as by-products, blessed Emily and me.

Dear Christian, consider how many opportunities each of us may have missed to become integral moving parts in His divine works, when distracted and driven by the lures of this world, the subtle whispers of our enemy, or the persistent cravings of our insatiable flesh. Or, as we repeatedly have shown here, being unaware the Lord was at work around us. Were we all willing to set aside but a small part of our daily consciousness to become ever-ready watchmen on His wall, waiters at His table, or on-call first responders to His every need, how much more might our lives be of use to bring Him glory and honor due His name by glorifying His works among men with God Stories, testimonies, and "Kisses from Heaven" from our own lives?

Yet, despite our failures, He has committed Himself to us for no valid reason beyond merciful redemption for reconciliation, given His only begotten Son to save us from His own wrath, and then kept a door open to His eternal presence by simply asking His very creation, humankind, to believe in Him as God. For that, this world mocks Him for acting as if He were God, persecutes His children for not approving sin or exalting sinners, and reliably takes vengeance against any person, place, or thing that tries to take away the lofty, self-exalted "final-say-in-all-things" that humans so often insist belongs to them alone but never to Him.

So why are we surprised or offended this world overflows with pain when He is ignored as our comforter, full of lies when He is the truth-giver, addictions when He is the deliverer, wickedness when He is our righteousness, depression when He is the joy-giver, peace when He is the prince of peace, love when He is the lover of our souls, and, sadly, on and on? Ultimately, must we not assign humankind's obstinate fallen nature and corporate unsaved soul as reasons for this sorrowful state?

Still, we can take heart, for there will always be a holy remnant among Christians in every setting who believe and long to become a recognized landing zone for His presence, lodging for His Holy Spirit, a vessel to disperse His mercy. When a body of believers, together as the Spirit-filled ecclesia, are hungry to see the lost of this world transformed into saints by His undeserved salvation of grace (unmerited favor), we will see many healed, delivered, and set free from the prison of sin-soaked lives.

And because He will never deny Himself the opportunity to be a good Father (Abba), brotherly Son (Jesus), and companion friend (Holy Spirit), He does all He can to integrate His life with all humanity willing to receive it while pouring out "Kisses from Heaven" to convince us to trust Him, to believe His Word, and to prove His gospel by way of those unique, inexplicable, extraordinary, or supernatural testimonies (often God Stories like you have recently digested from this book) to the remainder of humankind.

If you already know Him intimately, then you have had a spiritual encounter with the God of the Universe, understand His marvelous ways, and have gleaned encouragement from this little tome of Kisses from Heaven. If you do not know Him and wish to open your life to His love, intimacy, and wonders, merely ask Jesus, and He will take you into a new way of life by way of a new birth, this time a spiritual one from Heaven. So if you make His way the best decision of your life (to be followed by your first Kiss from Heaven), take time beforehand to understand, believe in your heart, and, finally, confess with faith to the courts of Heaven what you are about to read aloud below.

> Dear Father in Heaven, I believe that Jesus is the Son of God and came in loving obedience to take full punishment for all my sins so you, Father, could forgive and welcome me into your family as your child. I believe you raised Jesus from the dead so I, too, might walk in the newness of life according to your promise: "If any man is in Christ, He is a new creature; the old things passed away; behold, new things have come" (2 Cor. 5:17).

> So, Father, as I have confessed Jesus as Lord and believe that You raised Him from the dead, I now receive your forgiveness, your Son's salvation, and my new life in the Spirit. Thank you, Father, thank you, Jesus, and thank you, Holy Spirit, in whose names I pray. Amen.

Dear Saint, Welcome to the Kingdom of Heaven and to the Church of the Living God! So blessed to know and love you with the love of our Lord, who lives within us by His Spirit, through us to fulfill His purposes, and aims to be our best friend and mentor.

In Jesus,
Caleb and Emily

Enjoy the following preview of
Kisses from Heaven
Book Two

A Peterbilt Surprise

(an excerpt from *Kisses from Heaven, Book Two*)

This Monday had been no different. Eyes full of sleep and body crying for just one more horizontal moment, I stumbled downstairs to the kitchen for a jolt of leaded java before leaving for the office. Ferried by their "swimmer mom" to early practice, the kids left me alone to inadequately console our five dogs. Weekends, gratefully, were set aside for family, although the children complained that Saturday swim meets, home-based work parties, or Sunday church services devoured them before they could get a taste.

The weekend in my rearview mirror and running a little late, with "McDonald hot" cup of coffee in hand, I flew out the door and into my veteran, somewhat wrinkled but reliable, brown stick-shift Chevy Suburban. Rolling down the driveway as a preface to entering Government Road, I marveled, as I did most mornings, at the glorious expanse of Dorena Reservoir stretched out lazily to the north, fog rising from her somber and still slumbering surface. "At least someone was getting a little rest," was my hackneyed retort before thanking the Lord for this breathtaking way to build a grateful heart for His creation before starting another hectic day in mine.

Slicing through a dense forest of giant Douglas firs, Government Road was little more than a reworked rural paved logging path with few shoulders or guard rails to shield a vehicle from its very sudden turns and steep embankments. That day, like most Oregon winter days, was dark, drab, wet, and chilly. The highway was slick, so I lingered at the mouth of our driveway until a loaded log truck on the way upriver to the Stewart mill thundered past, shaking "road wash" all over Big Brown before we took the road. Heading northwest while working my way through the old boy's gears to settle him into an easy fifty-miles-per-hour cruise, I put in my favorite Reba Rambo cassette (Anyone remember Reba?).

A parade of mill-bound log trucks flew by, heading in the opposite direction, each rudely disturbing the Suburban with windy backlashes and more mini showers purloined from the wet roadway. Within minutes, we approached the former Young Life Christian Camp, strategically situated a couple hundred feet from a blind curve marking the final descent from the reservoir's dam.

There was no advanced warning. None. Coming off that hill from the dam and plunging deeply out of control into the hairpin turn at its base was an empty log truck carrying its trailer, tires in a losing struggle to hold on to the greasy curve, and, sickeningly, as a squatter occupying Big Brown's and my entire lane. For Brown and I, there was no wiggle room. The fog line to our right was less than two feet from a treacherous unguarded thirty feet of near vertical drop into old-growth timber, which left no shoulder for any evasive maneuvers. But there it was, a mighty Peterbilt, bearing down on us, fifty feet away and so close I could read the manufacturer's emblem on its grill.

"Well," I mused with unequivocal certainty, "here comes today's main event." Foot jammed upon the brake, Big Brown and I, hydroplaning along that rainswept highway, quickly dissolved what little time we had left by deliberating between a face-to-face meeting with the looming log truck or breaking the surly bonds of Earth with a short flight into a cavernous roadside abyss guarded by a legion of giant Douglas firs. It took no deliberation at all to see that either choice presented a one-way ticket to Heaven.

It was inexplicably, then, and in less than the blink of an eye, that our out-of-control gargantuan adversary, his grill nearly filling Brown's windshield and within "spittin' distance" of our unscheduled tete-a-tete, performed the inconceivable . . .

Read the rest of this story in Kisses from Heaven
Book Two, releasing Fall 2024.

About the Author

Following earlier years as a United States Naval aviator with VMA (Marine fixed wing attack squadron) 324 aboard the carrier USS Independence, CVA 62, patrolling the Mediterranean Sea and VMA 223 stationed in Chu Lai, South Vietnam during that conflict, C.B. Caleb Woodworth, M.D. then served as flight surgeon for the US Fighter Weapons School (Top Gun) in Miramar, California. After ten years of military service, Doctor Woodworth went on to serve as a rural general practitioner and emergency physician in small-town Oregon and later as award-winning Director of the Eugene Department of Veterans Affairs Clinic for another two decades.

With intercessor and medical phlebotomist wife Emily Anne, the couple has ministered over the last twenty-five years as ordained pastors and missionaries in restoration (inner healing) ministry throughout the states and various nations. Among struggling addicts seeking new lives in Jesus, the Woodworths presently act as on-call volunteers with Jimi and Ladonna Waggoner's anointed Crossroad's Recovery Ministry in Poplar Bluff, Missouri.

Then, Emily in her spare moments helps keep the ties that bind among the couples' blended family, friends, and the Church while bringing in the afflicted, wounded, and needy for Holy Spirit's healing care. The few moments of time left over finds soon-to-be Great Grandma Em busy doing crafts for gifts and living up to her reputation as the neighborhood's "cookie lady."

You will find Caleb's days reliably filled with chronicling the Lord's mysterious ways in the book series Kisses from Heaven, working with Emily in the couples' Face to Face and Listening Prayer ministries, and caring for gentle Skipper the horse and Pony the pony (elderly equines the couple serves as fellow squatters on Jerry and Sandra Murphy's Moriah Ranch in southeast Missouri). Then, coaxed by insistent roosters Buc and Buc-Buc to a morning's breakfast while keeping track of Mama Kitty and her ever-fluctuating multitude of feline progeny, it is time to give treats to a variety of local poochies making their daily rounds to say hello. Finally, being eternally nudged into action by overly loved Princess Peaches n' Cream Barksalot, their not-so-gracefully aging mostly Jack Russell terrier whose genes have been gratefully toned down by a competing history of pug and beagle, must be heralded, at least by her parents, as a daily Kiss from Heaven by herself.

Emily and Caleb doubt the Lord could be more gracious or life sweeter in their later years. But aren't they always ready, waiting, and hungry for another surprise Kiss from Heaven from their First Love, Jesus, and His Helper, Holy Spirit? We can all be certain of that.

To connect with the author or place an order for bulk copies, please visit http://www.kissesfromheavenbooks.com.